MCSE Test Success:
NT Server 4

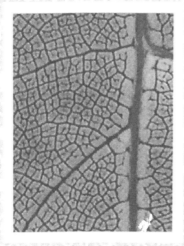

MCSE Test Success: NT® Server 4

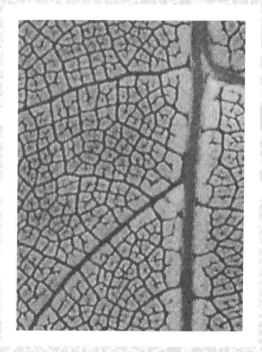

Lisa Donald

NETWORK PRESS®
SYBEX

San Francisco • Paris • Düsseldorf • Soest

Associate Publisher: Guy Hart-Davis
Contracts and Licensing Manager: Kristine Plachy
Acquisitions & Developmental Editor: Bonnie Bills
Editor: Alison Moncrieff
Technical Editor: Ron Reimann
Book Designers: Bill Gibson and Pat Dintino
Graphic Illustrator: Andrew Benzie
Electronic Publishing Specialist: Bill Gibson
Production Coordinator: Theresa Gonzalez
Production Assistant: Beth Moynihan
Indexer: Ted Laux
Cover Design: Archer Design

Screen reproductions produced with Collage Complete.

Collage Complete is a trademark of Inner Media Inc.

Sybex, Network Press, and the Network Press logo are registered trademarks of SYBEX Inc.

TRADEMARKS: SYBEX has attempted throughout this book to distinguish proprietary trademarks from descriptive terms by following the capitalization style used by the manufacturer.

The author and publisher have made their best efforts to prepare this book, and the content is based upon final release software whenever possible. Portions of the manuscript may be based upon pre-release versions supplied by software manufacturer(s). The author and the publisher make no representation or warranties of any kind with regard to the completeness or accuracy of the contents herein and accept no liability of any kind including but not limited to performance, merchantability, fitness for any particular purpose, or any losses or damages of any kind caused or alleged to be caused directly or indirectly from this book.

SYBEX is an independent entity from Microsoft Corporation, and not affiliated with Microsoft Corporation in any manner. This publication may be used in assisting students to prepare for a Microsoft Certified Professional Exam. Neither Microsoft Corporation, its designated review company, nor SYBEX warrants that use of this publication will ensure passing the relevant exam. Microsoft is either a registered trademark or trademark of Microsoft Corporation in the United States and/or other countries.

Library of Congress Card Number: 97-61721
ISBN: 0-7821-2148-9

Manufactured in the United States of America

10 9 8 7 6 5 4 3 2 1

For all of the want-to-be MCSEs.
Especially Brad.
Go take your tests!

Acknowledgments

This Test Success Guide has been a great book to work on. I want to start by thanking Bonnie Bills of Sybex for involving me in this project. Between the Sybex Study Guides and the Test Success books, I am feeling very intimate with the MCSE exams. It's great to have a chance to share this information through these projects. Bonnie was great to work with and allowed me to do the job to the best of my ability.

I also want to thank my editor, Alison Moncrieff, who always does a great job in addition to being a wonderful person to work with. Ron Reimann worked on this book as the technical editor. Thanks to Ron for his hard work and technical savvy.

The Sybex production team—Production Coordinator Theresa Gonzalez, Electronic Publishing Specialist Bill Gibson, Graphic Illustrator Andrew Benzie, and Indexer Ted Laux—also did a great job. Thanks to everyone for their hard work.

Finally, thanks to my family and friends for being so understanding, even as I was stressing out again over deadlines.

Contents at a Glance

Table of Contents

Introduction

One of the greatest challenges facing corporate America is finding people who are qualified to manage corporate computer networks. One of the most common operating systems is Windows NT. As you already know, Windows NT is not a trivial operating system and requires skill and knowledge to manage. To show that a certain level of knowledge has been attained, Microsoft has a certification program that shows employers that someone who has Microsoft certification is capable of managing complex NT networks. The most highly coveted certification is MCSE or Microsoft Certified Systems Engineer.

Why become an MCSE? The main benefit is that you will have much greater earning potential and it carries high industry recognition. Certification can be your key to a new job, or a higher salary—or both.

So what's stopping you? If it's because you don't know what to expect from the tests or are worried that you might not pass, then this book is for you.

Your Key to Passing Exam 70-067

This book provides you with the key to passing Exam 70-067, Implementing and Supporting Windows NT Server 4.0. Inside, you'll find all the information relevant to this exam, including information on some of the "picky" questions on less frequently used options, and hundreds of practice questions.

Understand the Exam Objectives

This book is structured according to the MCSE NT Server exam objectives. At-a-glance review sections and 370 review questions bolster your knowledge of the information relevant to each objective and the exam itself. You learn exactly what you need to know without wasting time on tangents that are not covered by the exam. This book prepares you for the *exam* in the shortest amount of time possible, although to be ready for the real world you need to study the subject in greater depth and get a lot of hands-on practice.

Get Ready for the Real Thing

More than 125 sample test questions prepare you for the test-taking experience. These are multiple-choice questions that resemble actual exam questions—some are even more difficult than what you'll find on the exam. If you can pass the Sample Tests at the end of each unit and the Final Exam at the end of the book, you'll know you're ready.

Is This Book for You?

This book is intended for those who already have some experience with NT Server. It is especially well-suited for:

- Students using courseware or taking a course to prepare for the exam, and who need to supplement their study material with test-based practice questions.

- Network engineers who have worked with the product, but still need to fill in some holes.

- Anyone who has studied for the exams—using self-study guides, computer-based training, classes, or on the job—and wants to make sure that they're adequately prepared.

Understanding Microsoft Certification

Microsoft offers several levels of certification for anyone who has or is pursuing a career as a network professional working with Microsoft products:

- Microsoft Certified Professional (MCP)

- Microsoft Certified Systems Engineer (MCSE)

- Microsoft Certified Professional + Internet

- Microsoft Certified Systems Engineer + Internet

- Microsoft Certified Trainer (MCT)

The one you choose depends on your area of expertise and your career goals.

Microsoft Certified Professional (MCP)

This certification is for individuals with expertise in one specific area. MCP certification is often a stepping stone to MCSE certification and allows you some benefits of Microsoft certification after just one exam.

By passing one core exam (meaning an operating system exam), you become an MCP.

Microsoft Certified Systems Engineer (MCSE)

This is the certification for network professionals. By becoming an MCSE you differentiate yourself from an MCP. This certification is similar to a college degree in that it shows that you can make a commitment to complete all of the steps required for certification and that you meet high standards in being able to successfully complete all of the required exams.

To become an MCSE, you must pass a series of six exams:

1. Networking Essentials (waived for Novell CNEs)

2. Implementing and Supporting Microsoft Windows NT Workstation 4.0 (or Windows 95)

3. Implementing and Supporting Microsoft Windows NT Server 4.0

4. Implementing and Supporting Microsoft Windows NT Server 4.0 in the Enterprise

5. Elective

6. Elective

The following list applies to the NT 4.0 track. Microsoft still supports a track for 3.51, but 4.0 certification is more desirable because it is the current operating system.

Some of the electives include:

- Internetworking with Microsoft TCP/IP on Microsoft Windows NT 4.0

- Implementing and Supporting Microsoft Internet Information Server 4.0

- Implementing and Supporting Microsoft Exchange Server 5.5

- Implementing and Supporting Microsoft SNA Server 4.0

- Implementing and Supporting Microsoft Systems Management Server 1.2
- Implementing a Database Design on Microsoft SQL Server 6.5
- System Administration for Microsoft SQL Server 6.5

Microsoft Certified Trainer (MCT)

As an MCT, you can deliver Microsoft certified courseware through official Microsoft channels.

The MCT certification is more costly, because in addition to passing the exams, it requires that you sit through the official Microsoft courses. You also have to submit an application that must be approved by Microsoft. The number of exams you must pass depends on the number of courses you want to teach.

For the most up-to-date certification information, visit Microsoft's Web site at www.microsoft.com/train_cert.

Understanding Microsoft's Exam Objectives

In order to help you prepare for certification exams, Microsoft specifies a list of exam objectives for each test. These objectives are used to help you prepare for the exam. This book is based on the objectives.

For this exam the objectives were designed to measure your ability to design, administer, and troubleshoot NT Server 4.0 when it is part of an enterprise network. In this case an enterprise network is a network that spans a wide area network and consists of multiple domains.

Scheduling and Taking an Exam

Once you think you are ready to take an exam, call Prometric Testing Centers at (800) 755-EXAM (755-3926). They'll tell you where to find the closest testing center. Before you call, get out your credit card because each exam costs $100. (If you've used this book to prepare yourself thoroughly, chances are you'll only have to shell out that $100 once!)

You can schedule the exams for your convenience. The exams are downloaded from Prometric to the testing center, and you show up at your scheduled time and take the exam on a computer. Once you complete the exam, you will know right away whether you have passed or not. If you pass the exam, you don't need to do anything else—Prometric uploads the test results to Microsoft. If you don't pass, it's another $100 to schedule the exam again.

At the end of the exam, you will receive a score report. It will list the six areas that you were tested on and how you performed. Each unit in this book corresponds to one of the six main objectives. If you do not pass the exam, you will know from the score report where you did poorly, so you can study that particular unit in the Test Success book more carefully.

Test-Taking Hints

Get there early and be prepared This is your last chance to review. Bring your Test Success Book and review any areas you feel unsure of. Also be prepared to show two forms of ID. If you need a quick drink of water or a visit to the restroom, take the time before the exam. Once your exam starts, it will not be paused for these needs.

What you can and can't take in with you These are closed-book exams. The only thing that you can take in is scratch paper provided by the testing center. Use this paper as much as possible to diagram the questions. Many times diagramming questions will help make the answer clear. You will have to give this paper back to the test administrator at the end of the exam.

Many testing centers are very strict about what you can take into the testing room. Some testing centers have gone so far as to require that I can't even take in a zipped-up purse. If you feel tempted to take in any outside material, beware that many testing centers use monitoring devices such as video and audio equipment (so don't swear, even if you are alone in the room!).

Prometric Testing Centers take the test-taking process and the test validation very seriously.

What to expect When you arrive for your exam, you will be asked to present your ID. You will also be asked to sign a piece of paper that specifies that you understand the testing rules. An example is that you will not cheat on the exam.

Before you start the exam you will have an opportunity to take a practice exam. It is not related to NT and is used so that you will have a feel for the exam process.

Then you will take the exam. When you are done with the exam, you will receive your score report. You will also have an opportunity to evaluate the exam and the testing center.

Test approach   This really depends on the type of test taker you are. I'm of the school that believes you either know the answer or you don't. If you know the answer, answer the question and move on. If you are not sure of the answer, mark your best guess, then "mark" the question. At the end of the exam, you can view all of your answers or only the questions you have marked. Depending on the amount of time remaining, you can then view all of the questions again, or you view only the questions you were unsure of. I always like to double check all of my answers, because sometimes I misread the question on the first pass. I also find that a related question might provide the answer for a question that I may have been unsure of.

Be sure to answer all questions. Unanswered questions are scored as incorrect and will count against you. Make sure that you keep an eye on the remaining time so that you can pace yourself accordingly.

One piece of advice: If you have narrowed down the answers to two options, always go with your gut reaction, it is usually correct.

If you do not pass the exam, note everything that you can remember while the exam is still fresh on your mind. This will help you prepare for your next exam. Many times the questions overlap, and you don't want to miss the same questions again.

After You Become Certified

Once you become an MCSE, Microsoft kicks in some goodies, including:

- A one-year subscription to Microsoft Technet, a valuable CD collection that contains Microsoft support information

- A one-year subscription to the Microsoft Beta Evaluation program, which is a great way to get your hands on new software. Be the first kid on the block to play with new and upcoming software.

- Access to a secured area of the Microsoft Web site that provides technical support and product information. This certification benefit is also available for MCP certification.

- Permission to use the Microsoft Certified Professional logos (each certification has its own logo), which look great on letterhead and business cards

- An MCP certificate (you will get a certificate for each level of certification you reach), suitable for framing, or sending copies to Mom

- A one-year subscription to Microsoft Certified Professional Magazine, which provides information on professional and career development

Preparing for the MCSE Exams

To prepare for the MCSE certification exams, you should try to work with the product as much as possible. In addition, there are a variety of resources from which you can learn about the products and exams.

Courses

Instructor-Led Be very careful when choosing instructor-led courses. The Microsoft training materials do not always have a high correlation with the exam objectives. If your primary goal is to pass the certification exams, this book is an excellent resource because it will fill in holes left by the Microsoft courseware.

Online Online training is an alternative to instructor-led training. This is a useful option for people who are limited geographically from attending instructor-led training.

Self-Study Guides

If you prefer to use a book to help you prepare for the MCSE tests, you'll find a wide variety available, from complete study guides (such as the Network Press MCSE Study Guide series, which cover the core MCSE exams and key electives) through test-preparation books similar to this one.

For more MCSE information, go to the Sybex Web site. There, you'll find information about the MCP program, useful links, and descriptions of the other quality books in Sybex's MCSE line. Point your browser to http://www.sybex.com, and from the home page click on the MCSE logo.

How to Use This Book

This book is designed to help you prepare for the MCSE exam. It reviews each objective and relevant test-taking information, then you have a chance to test your knowledge through Study Questions and a Sample Test.

For each unit:

1. Review the exam objectives list at the beginning of the unit. (You may want to check the Microsoft Train_Cert Web site to make sure the objectives haven't changed.) There are six main objectives. They include:

   A. Planning

   B. Installation and Configuration

   C. Managing Resources

   D. Connectivity

   E. Monitoring and Optimization

   F. Troubleshooting

2. Depending on your level of expertise, read through or scan the reference material that follows the objectives list. Broken down according to the objectives, this section helps you brush up on the information you need to know for the exam.

3. Review your knowledge in the Study Questions section. These are straightforward questions designed to test your knowledge of the specified topic. Answers to Study Questions are listed in the Appendix at the back of the book.

4. Once you feel sure of your knowledge of the area, take the Sample Test. The Sample Test is formatted in content and style to match the real exam. Instead of asking the "cut and dried" questions, you are presented with more scenario-based questions. This will help prepare you for the real exam. Sometimes, half of the battle is in trying to figure out exactly what the question is asking you. Set yourself a time limit based on the number of questions: A general rule is that you should be able to answer 20 questions in 30 minutes. When you've finished, check your answers with the Appendix in the back of the book. If you answer at least 85% of the questions correctly within the time limit (the first time you take the Sample Test), you're in good shape. To really prepare, you should note the questions you miss and be able to score 95-100% correctly on subsequent tries.

5. After you successfully complete Units 1-6, you're ready for the Final Exam in Unit 7. Allow yourself 90 minutes to complete the test of 55 questions. If you answer 85% of the questions correctly on the first try, you're well prepared. If not, go back and review your knowledge of the areas you struggled with, and take the test again.

6. Right before you take the test, scan the reference material at the beginning of each unit to refresh your memory.

At this point, you are well on your way to becoming certified!

Good Luck!

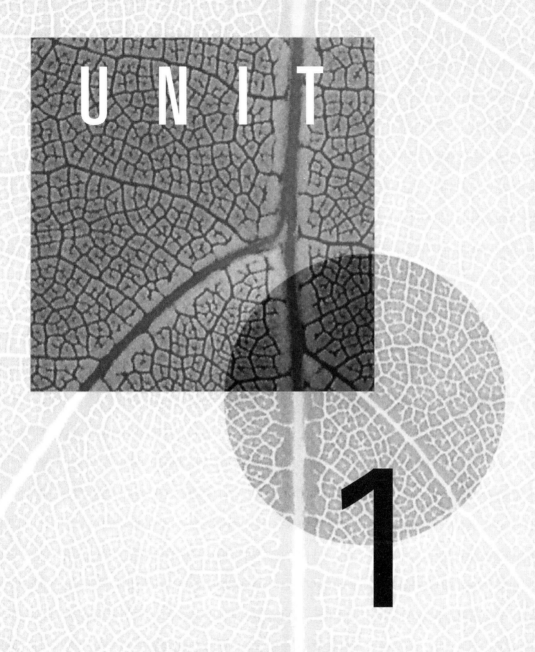

UNIT

1

Planning

Test Objectives: Planning

- Plan the disk drive configuration for various requirements. Requirements include:

  - Choosing a file system
  - Choosing a fault-tolerance method

- Choose a protocol for various situations. Protocols include:

  - TCP/IP
  - NWLink IPX/SPX Compatible Transport
  - NetBEUI

Exam objectives are subject to change at any time without prior notice and at Microsoft's sole discretion. Please visit Microsoft's Training & Certification website (www.microsoft.com/Train_Cert) for the most current exam objectives listing.

Planning involves selecting the correct disk drive configuration and being able to choose the protocol that is right for your environment.

Planning Disk Drive Configurations

Planning your disk drive configurations involves choosing the correct file system and selecting the best fault-tolerance option for your environment.

Choosing the Correct File System

NT supports three file systems:

- File Allocation Table (FAT)

- New Technologies File System (NTFS)

NT allows use of the long file-naming convention that appears in VFAT on Win 95 and DOS 7. You can have 255 characters and use spaces and periods in ways not allowed before.

FAT and NTFS are compared in Table 1.1.

TABLE 1.1	FAT	NTFS
FAT vs. NTFS	Supports long file names (file names can be up to 255 characters and contain spaces and multiple periods)	Supports long file names
	Accessible from all major operating systems	Not accessible from other operating systems

T A B L E 1.1 *(cont.)* FAT vs. NTFS	FAT	NTFS
	No local security available	Offers local security through permissions, auditing, and ownership
	Does not support file compression	Supports file compression
	Does not support Macintosh files	Only system to allow creations of Macintosh accessible volumes
	Maximum of 4GB	Maximum of 16 Exabytes

Choosing the Correct Tolerance Option

Plan your disk drive configurations carefully, as they will determine performance and fault tolerance for your computer. NT supports many different configurations. Three possible configurations are:

- Disk striping
- Disk mirroring
- Disk striping with parity

Disk Striping

Disk striping, or RAID 0, uses between two and 32 drives in a stripe set (see Figure 1.1).

Advantage

- Striping data over multiple disk channels improves performance on disk reads and writes.

Disadvantages

- No parity information is stored.
- If any drive in the stripe set fails, you lose all access to the stripe set.
- The system and boot partition cannot be a part of a stripe set.

FIGURE 1.1

Disk Striping

Disk striping spreads data evenly over the stripe
set in 64K increments.

Disk Mirroring

Disk mirroring, or RAID 1, is used to mirror one physical partition to a separate physical partition. Disk mirroring (see Figure 1.2) uses one physical controller which drives two physical hard drives. Disk duplexing (see Figure 1.3) is
a variation of disk mirroring, in that it provides additional redundancy by
using separate and independent controllers and hard drives for each logical
drive. Although not required, it is recommended that you use identical hard
drives and controllers.

Advantages

- If one of your drives fails, the other drive will continue to function
  without a service interruption.

- This is the only fault tolerant configuration that can be used on system
  and boot partitions.

- Disk read operations are faster than those on a single disk partition,
  which may result in faster read performance.

Disadvantages

- There is 100% disk overhead on disk mirroring, meaning if you are using
  two 2GB drives in your mirror set, only 2GB is available for data, the
  other 2GB is an exact duplicate of the data.

- Write operations may be slightly slower than normal since the data is
  written simultaneously to both disk drives.

- It is expensive to implement since hardware is doubled for a given storage
  capacity.

FIGURE 1.2

Disk Mirroring

Disk mirroring involves one controller, two disks.

FIGURE 1.3

Disk Duplexing

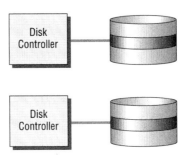

Disk duplexing involves two controllers, two disks.

Disk Striping with Parity

Disk striping with parity, or RAID 5, is similar to disk striping, except that mathematical calculations are performed and stored as parity information striped across the drives in the array.

Advantages

- If one drive fails, the data can be reconstructed from the parity on the surviving drives in the array.

- You can use the NT implementation of RAID 5 on an array of 3 to 32 drives.

- With RAID 5, you get more data capacity than you do with RAID 1, which uses the same size partition for data and mirroring. With RAID 5, you basically lose the sum of one drive. For example, an array with four 100MB drives would allow 300MB for data and 100MB for parity.

- All disks in the array can perform read operations simultaneously, resulting in faster read performance.

- It is typically cheaper than a mirror set.

Disadvantages

- While the failed drive is being replaced through parity information, system performance will be very slow.

- The system and boot partition cannot be a part of a stripe set.

- Write operations are slower. This makes it unsuitable for servers that for example continuously update large databases.

Choosing Protocols

When installing NT Server, you can choose from three primary network protocols:

- TCP/IP

- NWLink (Microsoft IPX/SPX Compatible Transport)

- NetBEUI

These protocols are compared in Table 1.2.

T A B L E 1.2 Protocols Compared	**TCP/IP**	**NWLink**	**NetBEUI**
	Suite of related protocols developed by DARPA	Based on Novell's proprietary IPX/SPX transport protocol	Implements the NetBIOS frame transport protocol
	Slightly slower than NWLink and much slower than NetBEUI	Faster than current NT implementation of TCP/IP, but much slower than NetBEUI	Very fast on small networks
	Relatively high overhead to support seamless connectivity and routing	Slightly lower overhead than TCP/IP, but does not offer all of the features of TCP/IP	Requires little overhead
	Routable	Routable	Not routable

T A B L E 1.2 *(cont.)* Protocols Compared	**TCP/IP**	**NWLink**	**NetBEUI**
	Supports features like DHCP and WINS	Supports routing	No routing support
	Used in most networks, especially if Internet connectivity is required	Used when compatibility with NetWare networks is required	Used in small, departmental LANs
	Requires the most configuration (IP address, subnet mask, and default gateway)	Requires configuration of frame type in some situations (supports auto-detection of frame type)	Requires no configuration

Planning Disk Drive Configurations

1. With disk _____ you use a redundant data channel through two disk controllers and two hard drives.

2. With disk _____ you use a redundant data channel through a single disk controller and two hard drives.

3. _____ is the only disk drive configuration that provides fault tolerance for the system or boot partition.

4. Assume that you are using five drives in a stripe set with parity. Each drive consists of 500MB. How much disk space will be used for data and how much disk space will be used to store parity information?

Disk space _____

Parity information _____

5. Disk mirroring is considered RAID _____.

6. Disk striping with parity is considered RAID _____.

7. In a stripe set, you can have a minimum of _____ drives and a maximum of _____ drives.

8. In a stripe set with parity, you can have a minimum of _____ _____ drives and a maximum of _____drives.

9. True or False. The following levels of RAID are supported through NT.

RAID 0 _____

RAID 1 _____

RAID 2 _____

RAID 3 _____

RAID 4 _____

RAID 5 _____

10. You are installing NT Server and need to choose a file system. List four advantages of using the NTFS file system.

_____

_____

_____

_____

11. What is the main advantage of using the FAT file system over NTFS?

_____

12.   Which file system(s) can be used with the following levels of RAID?

RAID 0 _____

RAID 1 _____

RAID 5 _____

Choosing Protocols

13.   The _____ and _____
_____ protocols are good choices in an enterprise network because they are routable.

14.   The _____ protocol is the fastest and most efficient
protocol that can be selected during the installation of NT Server.

15.   The _____ protocol is used with TCP/IP for automatic
configuration of clients.

16.   If TCP/IP is configured manually, which three options must be configured?

_____

_____

_____

17. List the two options that can be configured for NWLink IPX/SPX Compatible Transport.

_____

_____

18. The _____ protocol is required if you will be accessing the Internet.

19. The _____ protocol is normally used in connection with networks that contain a mixture of NT and NetWare.

20. The _____ protocol would be used to support a mixed environment that contained NT and UNIX machines.

1-1   Your company is in the process of selecting a disk configuration for a server that will be used as the company's applications server. You have been given the following criteria:

Required: The disk configuration must be fault tolerant

Optional: The disk configuration must provide high performance

The disk configuration should support the system and boot partition

You decide to use disk striping. What components are met through this solution?

A. It meets the required requirement and both of the optional requirements.

B. It meets the required requirement and one optional requirement.

C. It doesn't meet the required requirement, but it meets both optional requirements.

D. It doesn't meet the required requirement, but it meets one optional requirement.

E. It doesn't meet the required requirement or the optional requirements.

1-2   Which of the following statements is true of NWLink IPX/SPX Compatible Transport?

A. It is NDIS compliant to Novell's IPX/SPX protocol stack.

B. It is a 32-bit protocol stack.

C. It provides support for NetBIOS.

D. It allows NT computers to access NetWare resources.

1-3   Which frame type is preferred if you choose to auto-detect frame type when configuring NWLink IPX/SPX Compatible Transport?

A. Ethernet_802.2

B. Ethernet_802.3

C. Ethernet_SNAP

D. Ethernet_II

1-4   Which statement(s) reflect the capabilities of NetBEUI?

    A. It uses self-configuration and self-tuning.

    B. It uses a small memory overhead.

    C. It is routable.

    D. It provides connection oriented and connectionless communication.

1-5   Your company is in the process of selecting a disk configuration for a server that will be used as the company's applications server. You have been given the following criteria:

    Required: The disk configuration must be fault tolerant

    Optional: The disk configuration must provide high performance

            The disk configuration should support the system and boot partition

You decide to use disk mirroring. What components are met through this solution?

    A. It meets the required requirement and both of the optional requirements.

    B. It meets the required requirement and one optional requirement.

    C. It doesn't meet the required requirement, but it meets both optional requirements.

    D. It doesn't meet the required requirement, but it meets one optional requirement.

    E. It doesn't meet the required requirement or the optional requirements.

1-6   Your company is in the process of selecting a disk configuration for a server that will be used as the company's applications server. You have been given the following criteria:

    Required: The disk configuration must be fault tolerant

    Optional: The disk configuration must provide high performance

            The disk configuration should support the system and boot partition

You decide to use striping with parity. What components are met through this solution?

    A. It meets the required requirement and both optional requirements.

    B. It meets the required requirement and one optional requirement.

C. It doesn't meet the required requirement, but it meets both optional requirements.

D. It doesn't meet the required requirement, but it meets one optional requirement.

E. It doesn't meet the required requirement or the optional requirements.

1-7 Which options provide fault tolerance for the system and boot partition? Choose all that apply.

A. Disk striping

B. Disk mirroring

C. Disk duplexing

D. Disk striping with parity

1-8 What is the minimum disk configuration required for disk striping with parity?

A. Two drives, each with a parity stripe

B. Three drives, each with a parity stripe

C. Two drives, one is reserved as a parity drive

D. Three drives, one is reserved as a parity drive

1-9 Which fault tolerance option would provide the highest level of fault tolerance on a system and boot partition?

A. Disk striping

B. Disk mirroring

C. Disk duplexing

D. Disk striping with parity

SAMPLE TEST

1-10 Which utility would you use to configure disk mirroring?

    A. SETUP

    B. Disk Manager

    C. Disk Administrator

    D. FDISK

1-11 You have four drives in your stripe set with parity, each drive is 1GB in size. How much space will be available to store data?

    A. 4GB

    B. 3.5GB

    C. 3GB

    D. 2.5GB

1-12 You have four drives in your stripe set, each drive is 1GB in size. How much space will be available to store data?

    A. 4GB

    B. 3.5GB

    C. 3GB

    D. 2.5GB

1-13 You have been asked to choose a file system for your new server. You have been given the following criteria:

    Required: The file system must support local security

    Optional: The file system should support Macintosh volumes

        The file system should be accessible through Windows 95 since the computer is configured with a dual-boot configuration

        The file system should support file compression

You decide to use NTFS. What components are met through this solution?

A. It meets the required requirement and all three of the optional requirements.

B. It meets the required requirement and one optional requirement.

C. It meets the required requirement and two optional requirements.

D. It doesn't meet the required requirement, but it meets two optional requirements.

E. It doesn't meet the required requirement, but it meets one optional requirement.

F. It doesn't meet the required requirement or the optional requirements.

1-14   You have been asked to choose a file system for your new server. You have been given the following criteria:

Required: The file system must support local security

Optional: The file system should support Macintosh volumes

The file system should be accessible through Windows 95 since the computer is configured with a dual-boot configuration

The file system should support file compression

You decide to use FAT. What compoare met through this solution?

A. It meets the required requirement and all three of the optional requirements.

B. It meets the required requirement and one optional requirement.

C. It doesn't meet the required requirement, but it meets two optional requirements.

D. It doesn't meet the required requirement, but it meets one optional requirement.

E. It doesn't meet the required requirement or the optional requirements.

1-15 You are installing an NT server with four physical hard drives. Each drive is identical. You want to achieve the highest performance possible with the maximum amount of storage. Which disk configuration should you choose?

   A. Disk striping

   B. Disk mirroring

   C. Disk duplexing

   D. Disk striping with parity

1-16 You are installing an NT server with four physical hard drives. Each drive is identical. You want to achieve the highest performance possible with the maximum amount of storage, however you are also concerned with fault tolerance. Which disk configuration should you choose?

   A. Disk striping

   B. Disk mirroring

   C. Disk duplexing

   D. Disk striping with parity

1-17 Your computer is configured with two SCSI adapters and two SCSI hard drives. You have been asked to install the server and choose a disk configuration with fault tolerance in mind. Which disk configuration is the best option?

   A. Disk mirroring

   B. Disk replicating

   C. Disk striping with parity

   D. Disk duplexing

1-18   What is the minimum number of disk drives that can be used in a stripe set?

    A. Two

    B. Three

    C. Four

    D. Five

1-19   What is the minimum number of disk drives that can be used in a stripe set with parity?

    A. Two

    B. Three

    C. Four

    D. Five

1-20   You have been using the FAT file system, but have decided that the NTFS file system would better suit your needs. You want to preserve your existing data. Which of the following utilities could you use?

    A. Disk Administrator

    B. FORMAT *drive letter*: /NTFS

    C. CONVERT

    D. FDISK

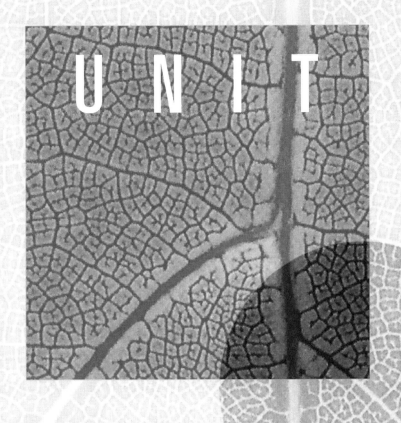

UNIT

2

Installation and Configuration

Test Objectives: Installation and Configuration

- Install Windows NT Server on Intel-based platforms.

- Install Windows NT Server to perform various server roles. Server roles include:
  - Primary domain controller
  - Backup domain controller
  - Member server

- Install Windows NT Server by using various methods. Installation methods include:
  - CD-ROM
  - Over-the-network
  - Network Client Administrator
  - Express versus Custom

- Configure protocol and protocol bindings. Protocols include:
  - TCP/IP
  - NWLink IPX/SPX Compatible Transport
  - NetBEUI

- Configure network adapters, Considerations include:
  - Changing IRQ, IObase, and memory addresses
  - Configuring multiple adapters

- ▨ Configure Windows NT Server core services. Services include:
  - Directory Replicator
  - License Manager
  - Other services

- ▨ Configure peripherals and devices. Peripherals and devices include:
  - Communication devices
  - SCSI devices
  - Tape device drivers
  - UPS devices and UPS service
  - Mouse drivers, display drivers, and keyboard drivers

- ▨ Configure hard disks to meet various requirements. Requirements include:
  - Allocating disk space capacity
  - Providing redundancy
  - Improving performance
  - Providing security
  - Formatting

- ▨ Configure printers. Tasks include:
  - Adding and configuring a printer
  - Implementing a printer pool
  - Setting print priorities

- Configure a Windows NT Server computer for various types of client computers. Client computers include:
  - Windows NT Workstation
  - Microsoft Windows 95
  - Microsoft MS-DOS based

 Exam objectives are subject to change at any time without prior notice and at Microsoft's sole discretion. Please visit Microsoft's Training & Certification web-site (www.microsoft.com/Train_Cert) for the most current exam objectives listing.

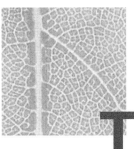

The following sections will cover the installation and configuration of NT Server.

Installing an Intel-Based Server

To install NT on an Intel x86 platform, use one of the following commands based on the existing operating system:

WINNT   Used to install NT from a computer where no operating system exists, or the computer is running a 16-bit operating system (including DOS, Windows 3.*x*, WFW 3.*x* or Windows 95).

WINNT32   Used to upgrade NT from a previous version, because NT is a 32-bit operating system.

In addition, the following command-line switches should be noted:

/b   Performs the installation by loading the boot floppy files from the Installation source to the system hard drive removing the requirement to use the three boot floppy diskettes.

/ox   Creates the three boot floppy diskettes for CD-ROM or floppy based install.

To see a complete list of the WINNT and WINNT32 command line switches, type the WINNT command with the /? Switch.

As you go through the NT Server installation, you will be asked to define the role your server will play.

NT Server Roles

NT servers can be installed in three types of roles within an NT domain:

- Primary Domain Controller (PDC)
- Backup Domain Controller (BDC)
- Member Server

Primary Domain Controller

Each domain must have one, and only one, PDC. The PDC contains the user accounts database known as the Security Accounts Manager (SAM) for the domain. It is the only computer that contains a read-write database of the SAM, which is then copied to computers that act as BDCs.

Backup Domain Controller

A BDC offloads logon authentication from the PDC and provides fault tolerance in the event that the PDC becomes unavailable. The PDC receives automatic updates of the SAM from the PDC every five minutes or can be manually updated at any time.

Member Server

A member server is a server that does not contain the SAM database. This allows the server to act in a specialized capacity without the overhead of logon authentication and SAM synchronization. It may also be moved from any NT domain to another.

The server roles are compared in Table 2.1.

T A B L E 2.1:   Server Role Comparison

	PDC	BDC	Member Server
Number in Domain	One	None required, but you normally want at least one—you can have as many as you need	None required

T A B L E 2.1: Server Role Comparison *(Continued)*

	PDC	BDC	Member Server
Primary Purpose	Controls the NT Domain. Assumes role of Domain Master Browser. Contains the read-write SAM database	Contains a read-only copy of the SAM database, used to offload logon authentication and provide fault tolerance	Act as a dedicated file, print, or applications server
Switchable Roles	A PDC can become a BDC if a BDC is promoted, but not a member server without reinstallation	A BDC can become a PDC, but not a member server without reinstallation	A member server cannot become a PDC or BDC without reinstallation
Domain Hopping	A PDC cannot switch domains without reinstallation	A BDC cannot switch domains without reinstallation	A member server can change domains

Now that you have the information to select a server role, the next choice is to choose an installation method for NT Server.

Installation Methods for NT Server

NT Server can be installed using one of three methods as shown in Table 2.2.

T A B L E 2.2 Installation methods for NT Server	Method	When do you use it?	How do you use it?
	From the CD-ROM	This is used when installing a single server with a CD-ROM attached. It is the simplest install method for creating a single or small number of NT servers	Install directly from the CD-ROM using the WINNT or WINNT32 command

T A B L E 2.2 *(cont.)* Installation methods for NT Server	Method	When do you use it?	How do you use it?
	Over the network	Use this method for computers without CD drives attached or that use unsupported CD drives. The drawback is that it increases network traffic	Copy and share the installation media on a network server. The machine that you install NT Server onto must be connected to the network server and you start the installation from the shared directory that contains the installation files
	Through the Network Client Administrator	Use this method when you want to use the over-the-network installation method but need to connect to the server to access the installation files	Use the Network Client Administrator to create an installation boot disk that can be used to attach to the distribution server and then install NT Server over the network

With all of these methods, you can also choose an Express or Custom installation. Installation of large numbers of NT servers can be automated by using Unattended Answer Files (`unattend.txt`) and Uniqueness Difference Files (UDFs) in conjunction with the `WINNT` or `WINNT32` commands.

Express versus Custom Installation

When you install NT Server, you are prompted to select from an Express or Custom installation, compared in Table 2.3.

T A B L E 2.3 Express versus Custom Installation	Express	Custom
	Installs NT in the most common configuration (asking you the minimum number of questions)	Allows you to make more complex installation decisions

T A B L E 2.3 (cont.) Express versus Custom Installation	**Express**	**Custom**
	The setup program identifies and configures the hardware for you	You specify the hardware you are using and its configuration
	All NT common components are installed	You must select which components you want installed
	Only one network card is detected	You can install the drivers for multiple network cards and specify their configuration. Additional networking protocols can be installed
	`PAGEFILE.SYS` is automatically created	You can specify the exact size and location of `PAGEFILE.SYS`

Another option you have during server installation is selecting your protocols, configuring your protocols, and protocol bindings. These options will be covered in the next section.

Configuring Protocols and Protocol Bindings

The three protocols that you can choose from during the initial installation of NT Server are:

- TCP/IP
- NWLink IPX/SPX Compatible Transport
- NetBEUI

To view and configure these protocols, you use the Network applet within Control Panel.

TCP/IP

The TCP/IP protocol requires the most configuration of the three protocols. The TCP/IP configuration can be manual or automatic (see Figure 2.1). Table 2.4 compares the two installation types.

F I G U R E 2.1

The TCP/IP configuration screen

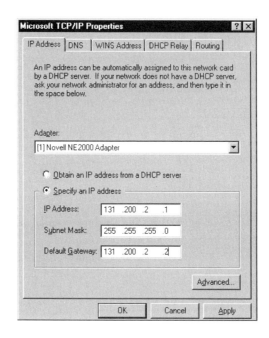

T A B L E 2.4

TCP/IP Manual and Automatic Configurations

Manual Configuration	Automatic Configuration
Does not require that a DHCP server be up and running	Requires a functional DHCP server be available
Requires you to configure an IP address, subnet mask, and default gateway (gateway is required only if routing outside subnet is needed)	Only requires you to select the Obtain An IP Address From A DHCP Server radio button
Must be changed manually every time the computer changes subnets	Automatically assigns the correct IP configuration information when a computer changes subnets

TABLE 2.4 *(cont.)*	**Manual Configuration**	**Automatic Configuration**
TCP/IP Manual and Automatic Configurations	Humans are more likely to make configuration errors that result in problems	Assuming that the DHCP server is setup correctly, many configuration problems are avoided
	More labor intensive for an administrator	Low administrative overhead for an administrator

NWLink IPX/SPX Compatible Transport

The NWLink IPX/SPX Compatible Transport protocol requires minimal configuration. The only configuration parameters are for Internal Network Number and Frame Type (see Figure 2.2).

FIGURE 2.2

The NWLink IPX/SPX Compatible Transport configuration screen

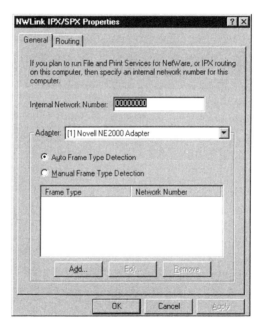

Internal Network Number

The Internal Network Number identifies a unique address that is used by NetWare. This is an optional configuration.

Use this option if:

- You are running File and Print Services for NetWare.

- You are using your NT Server as an IPX router.

If you will not be using the previous configurations, you should leave this filed at its default of eight zeros (00000000).

Frame Type

In order to communicate through NWLink, you must configure frame type. The frame type is associated with Ethernet transport protocols. You can choose from four Ethernet frame types, which are not compatible with each other and if the computers are not configured consistently, will not communicate with each other.

Instead of manually picking frame types, you can choose the Auto-detect option, which will prefer the Ethernet_802.2 frame type. If this frame type is not available, it will auto-detect the first frame type it detects.

If you are going to connect to resources that have more than one frame type, then all frame types must be entered manually during configuration.

NetBEUI

NetBEUI protocol does not require any configuration.

Binding Protocols

Binding is the linking of the physical adapter and NDIS driver to the network protocols and services that you are running. To access the bindings configuration and enable and disable bindings:

1. Select Control Panel ➤ Network, then choose the Binding tab. The Binding tab first lists all of the services that require network interaction.

2. Click on a service to see what protocols are bound to the service. The more commonly used protocols should be at the top of the binding list for better performance.

3. You can enable and disable bindings through this tab. You will have better network performance if you disable unnecessary bindings.

A topic closely related to protocols, is network adapters. The network adapter card must be configured properly or the protocols will not be able to access the network. In the next section, you will learn how network cards are configured.

Configuring Network Adapters

If you choose a default installation, your network adapter should be auto-detected. If there is a driver for your adapter on the NT Server distribution CD, it will be automatically loaded for you. If no driver exists, or you have a more updated driver, you can specify that you have a disk that will supply the driver.

Changing IRQ, Base I/O, and Memory Addresses

By default, NT will try and detect your network adapters hardware settings. Whatever setting your hardware is using, your NT configuration must match. Network adapters can be configured in a variety of ways including the following:

- Older cards may be set with jumpers or dip switches (these are pretty obsolete).

- Some cards are set through a software configuration program.

- Newer cards may auto-configure themselves to whatever configuration is available.

Consult the documentation that came with your network card to see how it should be configured. Once your adapter is configured and installed, NT will try and detect it during the installation. If it can detect and verify the settings, no further configuration is required.

If your card is not auto-configured properly:

1. Access Control Panel ➤ Network.

2. Select the Adapter tab. Your adapter should be displayed.

3. To change your network adapters settings, select the Properties tab (see Figure 2.3). From this screen you can change your configuration settings.

4. If the card is still not recognized, you may have to install manufacturer-supplied drivers or download drivers from the Microsoft or the vendors Web site.

FIGURE 2.3

The Network Card
setup screen

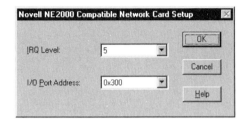

Depending on your network adapter, you may need to configure:

- IRQ

- Base memory address

- Base I/O address

- DMA

Configuring Multiple Adapters

If your NT server contains more than one network adapter card, it can be used as a router if the cards are on separate subnetworks. Configuring multiple adapters is very simple:

1. Configure and install the physical hardware.

2. Within Control Panel ➤ Network, select the Adapters tab.

3. You will see the Network Adapters configuration screen (see Figure 2.4). Simply click Add and supply the driver for your next adapter.

4. Configure the adapter as shown in the previous section.

Now that you have configured your protocols and network adapters, the next thing to consider is how you will configure your NT core services. This will include services such as the directory replicator, License Manager, and other services.

FIGURE 2.4

The Network Adapters
configuration screen

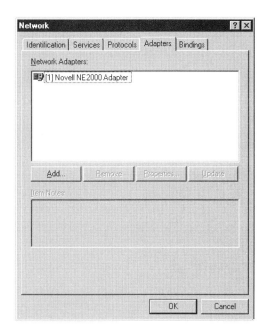

Configuring NT Server Core Services

This section will cover how to configure NT core services. This includes Directory Replicator, License Manager, and other services including NT Backup.

Directory Replicator

Directory replication is used to maintain exact directory structures on multiple computers. This is done by designating a computer as an export server (the one you're copying from) and another computer or computers as import servers (the one you're copying to). Directory replication is usually used to replicate read-only data like logon scripts and system policies to domain controllers within a domain.

The directory replicator service will only replicate directories and files in the WINNT\SYSTEM32\REPL\EXPORT directory. It will not replicate open files.

Requirements

- The export computer must be NT Server.

- The import computer can be NT Server or NT Workstation.

- The import and export computers must be running the directory replicator service.

- A user account must be created in the NT domain to allow the directory replicator service to run. The user account must be a part of the Replicator and Backup Operators group.

- Directory replication must be configured on the export and import computers through Server Manager.

License Manager

The License Manager is used to manage NT Server, Workstation, and other License Manager-aware application licenses. The idea is that you want to prevent having more users running applications than you have Client Access Licenses for. This ensures that the use of all of your software is legal. Through License Manager, you can track your NT Server and Client licenses. NT can be licensed per-server or per-seat.

Other Services

This section will cover the NT Backup service, NT Server service, and configuration of other NT services.

NT Backup

The Backup utility is accessed from the Administrative Tools Program group. It is a graphical utility used to back up NT files and directories to tape. You can back up FAT and NTFS partitions as well as the registry.

In addition the Backup program can back up shared drives that the server is connected to. This could include other NT Servers, NT Workstations, and Windows 95 clients. This makes Backup a network solution.

NT Backup can be automated by use of the AT command from the DOS command prompt.

NT Server Service

You can configure the NT Server service to be optimized for different environments. The options you can choose from are listed in Table 2.5.

T A B L E 2.5 NT Server Service configuration options	Option	Environment
	Minimize memory used	Choose this if you will be using the Server mainly as a workstation and you will have fewer than 10 connections to the server
	Balance	Choose this if you will be using Server as a workstation and a server and will support between 10 and 64 connections
	Maximize throughput for file sharing	Choose this if you are using your server as a domain controller or a file and print server
	Maximize throughput for network applications	Choose this if your server is being used to support distributed applications for memory caching, such as SQL server

To configure the NT Server service, choose Control Panel ➤ Network ➤ Services, click on Server Service, and click the Properties button.

NT Services

NT Services are processes that perform a specific system action or function. They can be configured through Control Panel ➤ Services or through Server Manager. Basically, you specify how you want the service to start and which account should be used to start the service.

The services that were just covered are not configured by default. However, if you have your peripherals and other devices installed prior to your installation of NT Server, they should be properly identified and configured during your installation. If they are installed after the installation, you can configure them as shown in the following section.

Configuring Peripherals and Devices

This section will cover how to configure communication devices, SCSI devices, tape device drivers, and mouse, display and keyboard drivers.

Communication Devices

NT supports communication devices such as modems. To configure a modem:

1. Use Control Panel ➤ Modems.

2. NT will try and detect and configure your modem for you.

3. If this is not possible, you can select or provide the driver for your modem.

SCSI Devices

SCSI stands for Small Computer Systems Interface. SCSI adapters can be used to connect devices such as hard drives, CD-ROM players, and printers. To define a SCSI device:

1. Use Control Panel ➤ SCSI Adapters.

2. Within the SCSI configuration screen, you can configure the device and driver you are using.

Tape Device Drivers

Tape devices are associated with backups. To install a tape device driver:

1. Choose Control Panel ➤ Tape Devices.

2. Your tape device should be detected and you then provide the appropriate driver.

UPS Devices and UPS Service

Uninterruptible Power Supplies, or UPSs, are used to provide power to your computer in the event of conventional power loss. To configure a UPS:

1. Use Control Panel ➤ UPS.

2. Then configure the settings as specified by your UPS vendor.

Mouse Drivers, Display Drivers, and Keyboard Drivers

To configure the listed drivers, use the following options in Control Panel.

Mouse drivers:	Mouse
Display drivers:	Display
Keyboard drivers	Keyboard

These drivers are all easy to install, and only require you to provide the correct source for the driver files.

Configuring hard disks is more involved. You must first select which configuration you will use, then implement it as described in the next section.

Configuring Hard Disks

You can configure your NT disks in many different configurations. Some of the options you can choose from include: volume sets, stripe sets, mirror sets, and stripe sets with parity. Each of these hard-disk configurations will determine what amount of disk space is available, redundancy of data, and performance.

Allocating Disk Space Capacity

You can allocate disk space in many ways. NT Server supports volume sets, stripe sets, mirror sets and stripe sets with parity; these are compared in Table 2.6.

T A B L E 2.6: NT Disk Configurations

	Volume Set	Stripe Set	Mirror Set	Stripe Set with Partity
Description	A volume set is disk space that spans more than one partition, but is recognized as a single volume, and has a single drive letter assigned to it	A stripe set combines disk space from multiple drives into a single logical drive. Data is written evenly across the stripe set	A mirror set is two partitions of equal size that mirror each other for redundancy	A stripe set with parity is similar to a stripe set, except that it contains parity information which is used for fault tolerance

T A B L E 2.6: NT Disk Configurations *(Continued)*

	Volume Set	Stripe Set	Mirror Set	Stripe Set with Partity
Requirements	2-32 drives, partitions can be any size	2-32 drives, partitions must be the same size	2 partitions, they must be the same size	3-32 drives, partitions must be the same size
Setup	A volume set can be initially created from free space through Disk Administrator. Volume sets can also be extended after initial creation through Disk Administrator. Extended volume sets must be NTFS	Stripe sets are created through Disk Administrator by selecting free space that is of equal size on multiple physical partitions. Once a stripe set has been created, it can be deleted, but not extended	To create a mirror set, you first create a partition, then select an area of free space on another partition that is equal to the first partition. From Disk Administrator, you then choose Establish Mirror	Stripe sets with parity are created by using Disk Administrator and selecting free space on three or more drives and choosing Create Stripe Set with Parity
Advantages	Volume sets allow you to extend available disk space when your drive is reaching capacity. You also have the advantage of combing partitions that are not the same size	Stripe sets increase performance by writing data evenly over two or more drives in a set. This also allows you to take advantage of multiple I/O channels	Mirror sets provide fault tolerance. If either drive fails, your system will continue to function. Mirror sets are also the only method of fault tolerance available for system and boot partitions	Stripe sets with parity provide fault tolerance by adding a parity stripe to each drive in the set
Disadvantages	In a volume set if any drive fails, the entire volume is unavailable	Stripe sets provide no fault tolerance, and if any drive fails, the entire set is unavailable	Only 50% of the space in a mirror set is available for data	If a drive fails, you can still access the data, but it is very slow. If two drives fail, you must rely on your backup
Usable Space for Data	All space is available for data	All space is available for data	Only 50% of the space in the mirror set is available for data	You lose the space of one drive partition in the stripe set that is used to store parity information

Providing Redundancy

NT Server has two disk configurations for providing redundancy, disk mirroring, and disk striping with parity. See Table 2.6 for an explanation of these two options.

Improving Performance

Performance can be increased through two disk drive configurations: disk striping and disk striping with parity. These options are covered in Table 2.6.

Providing Security

Security is provided through the NTFS file system. Once a partition has been formatted as NTFS you can assign file level permissions, audit usage, and specify ownership. This will be covered in greater detail in Unit 3.

Creation of NTFS Partition

You can create a NTFS partition through:

- The Disk Administrator utility

- The FORMAT command by using the following syntax
  FORMAT *drive letter*: /fs:NTFS

CONVERT

You can convert a FAT partition to a NTFS partition through the CONVERT command-line utility. The syntax is:

CONVERT *drive letter*: /fs:NTFS

Note that the CONVERT command-line utility is one-way. To go from NTFS back to FAT, you'd have to back up or copy the data to another location, re-format the drive as FAT, create a new partition, then restore the data from tape backup.

Formatting

In this section, we'll cover how disks are organized and formatted and how ARC naming conventions are established.

Organization and Formatting

Hard drives are organized into usable space through the creation of volumes. Once a volume has been created, it must be formatted with a file system such as FAT or NTFS.

ARC Naming Conventions

ARC stands for Advanced RISC Computing. ARC names are used in the BOOT.INI file to point to the location of the NT operating system. If you use default values, this is the \WINNT directory, and this partition is referred to as the boot partition. The ARC naming convention is as follows:

multi or scsi(x)disk(y)rdisk(z)partition(a)

These options are described in Table 2.7.

TABLE 2.7 ARC Naming Options Defined	Option	Description
	Multi(x) or SCSI(x)	The ARC name begins with either multi or scsi. Multi is used for any disk other than SCSI or a SCSI adapter that has its BIOS enabled. SCSI is used with SCSI controllers that have their BIOS disabled.
	Disk(x)	Used with the scsi option. If you used multi this number will always be 0. If you use scsi, this number will be the scsi bus number or target ID, this number will start with 0.
	Rdisk(x)	Used with the multi option. If you used scsi, this number will always be 0. For multi this number is the ordinal number of the disk and begins with 0.
	Partition(x)	Used with multi or scsi. This number is the ordinal number of the hard drive partition and always starts with 1.

Another important item that you will need to configure is printers. Printer configuration is covered in the next section.

Configuring Printers

$\mathbf{T}$his section will cover printer configuration. Specifically, you should know how to add and configure a printer, implement a printer pool, and set print priorities.

Adding and Configuring a Printer

This section will address how to add a printer, then configure a printer. Configuring most printers attached to a Domain computer running a DOS or Windows NT operating system is simple. Interfacing to network printers can be more complex to set up initially as DLC or TCP/IP shared network devices, but then are simple for users to connect to.

Remember the differences between a printer and print device in the Windows NT print model. A printer refers to a logical object within NT. A print device is the actual hardware device.

Adding a Printer

To add a printer:

1. Select Start ➢ Settings ➢ Printers.

2. NT uses a printer wizard that walks you through the process of installing a printer. The printer wizard will ask you to specify the options shown in Table 2.8.

T A B L E 2.8 Printer Wizard Configuration Selections	**Configuration Option**	**Description**
	My Computer or Network Print Server	My Computer assumes that you are configuring the printer for local or network access. The computer that you are defining the printer on automatically becomes that printers print server. If you choose Network Print Server, then the assumption is that you are attaching to an existing network printer

T A B L E 2.8 *(cont.)*	**Configuration Option**	**Description**
Printer Wizard Configuration Selections	Port	This defines the port that the printer is attached to. The port can be local or a network printer port
	Manufacturer and Printer	This option is used to specify your specific printer so that the correct driver can be selected
	Printer Name	Defines the printer's name. Through this screen you can also specify if this printer should be the user's default printer
	Shared or Not Shared	Shared implies that the printer is available for network access. Not shared means that it is only available to users of the local computer. If you choose shared, you can also configure the printer to support drivers for Windows 95, all Windows NT client versions, including non-Intel platforms. You also specify a share name

Configuring a Printer

Once a printer has been created under NT, you can configure it through the Printer Properties option. The six printer configuration tabs are defined in Table 2.9.

T A B L E 2.9	**Tab**	**Configuration Options**
Printer Tab Configuration Options	General	The General tab allows you to configure a comment, location, driver (can be used to update), separator page, print processor, and allows you to print a test page
	Ports	This is used to specify which port the printer is attached to. You can also add, delete, and configure ports through this tab
	Scheduling	Scheduling allows you to specify when a printer is available, the printers priority, and how print jobs should be spooled
	Sharing	This tab specifies whether or not a printer is shared. If the printer is shared, you can also specify a share name here, and which alternate drivers should automatically be available to remote users

	Tab	Configuration Options
T A B L E 2.9 *(cont.)* Printer Tab Configuration Options	Security	Used to configure permissions, ownership, and auditing.
	Device Settings	Configures printer-specific settings like tray assignment printer memory and font cartridges.

Implementing a Printer Pool

Printer pools (see Figure 2.5) are used to logically group print devices together, but yet only define a single printer. The benefit of a printer pool is that you can send your job to the logically defined printer, and the job will be sent to the first available print device.

F I G U R E 2.5

A printer pool

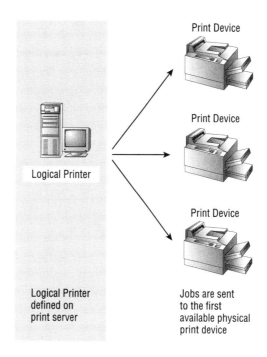

Print Device

Print Device

Print Device

Logical Printer

Logical Printer defined on print server

Jobs are sent to the first available physical print device

In order to create a printer pool, you must meet the following criteria:

- The print devices should be in close proximity, because the print job could go to any print device in the pool.

- The print devices must be able to use the same print driver.

Setting Print Priorities

Print priorities specify when a printer is available and its priority. The concept is the opposite of a printer pool. This concept assumes that you will have multiple logical printers that point to the same print device (see Figure 2.6).

FIGURE 2.6

Multiple logical printers pointing to a single print device

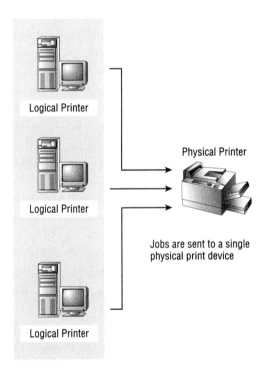

The following subsections define availability and priority.

Availability

Printers can be configured so that they are only available during a certain time period of the day.

Example: You define two printers, REPORTS and LASER, that point to the same laser printer. The REPORTS printer could be configured to only print between 12:00 and 6:00 AM while the LASER printer is available 24 hours a day. Users could then be directed to send jobs that are over 30 pages to the REPORTS printer so that the printer is not tied up with long jobs during the day.

Priority

Printers can be assigned priority between 1 and 99. 99 is the highest priority and 1 is the lowest priority.

Example: Assume that you have a printer called EXECS and a printer called ACCT that points to the same physical print device. You could assign permissions so that the EXECS group can use the EXECS printer and the ACCT group can use the ACCT printer. By giving the EXECS printer a priority of 99 and the ACCT printer a priority of 1, the EXECS printer will always submit its jobs first to the physical print device.

Now that you know how to configure NT printers, the next section will show you how to configure NT server for different clients.

Configuring NT Server for Various Clients

NT Server supports a variety of clients, including NT Workstation, Windows 95, and DOS-based clients.

Windows NT Workstation

NT Workstations must be configured to be part of the NT domain. To add a workstation to the domain:

1. Create a computer account for the workstation through Server Manager.

2. At the workstation, go to Control Panel ➤ Network, Identification tab. Specify the domain that the workstation should belong to.

Microsoft Windows 95

Windows 95 computers can be a part of an NT domain. Unlike NT Workstations, you do not configure Windows 95 clients through Server Manager. To configure the Windows 95 client to be a part of an NT domain, you take the following steps:

1. From Control Panel ➢ Network, choose the Configuration tab.

2. Add the Client Software for Microsoft Networks software.

3. After the software is installed, highlight Client Software for Microsoft Networks and click on the Properties button.

4. In the Properties dialog box, check Log on to Windows NT domain. Specify the domain that you will log on to.

Microsoft MS-DOS Based

DOS-based clients can also be a part of an NT domain. By default, DOS clients do not have networking software installed. To support DOS clients, you can use the Network Client Administrator to create an installation disk set for Network Client v3.0 for MS-DOS and Windows clients.

Installing an Intel-Based Server

1. What command starts the NT Server installation from a machine that currently has no operating system?

2. Assuming that the computer is running NT Server 3.51, and you want to upgrade it to NT Server 4.0, what command initiates the upgrade?

3. Which command and option would you use to start the NT Server installation on a computer running DOS without creating the three startup diskettes?

4. Which command and option would you use to create the three NT Server startup diskettes after the original installation has been completed? This assumes that you are at the computer that is running NT Server and that you have access to the Server CD.

5. True or False. You can upgrade NT Server 3.5 to NT 4.0 by using the WINNT32 command and installing NT 4.0 into the same directory that NT 3.5 was installed to.

6. True or False. You can upgrade Windows 95 to NT Server 4.0 by using the WINNT32 command and installing NT 4.0 into the same directory that Windows 95 was installed to.

7. During the installation of NT Server, your SCSI drive is not being recognized. What should you do?

_____

8. By default, NT Server will be installed into the _____ directory.

9. Which two file systems can be created and formatted during the installation of NT Server?

_____

_____

10. During the installation of NT Server, you are asked to supply a single, blank floppy disk. What is it used for?

_____

11. True or False. You can upgrade NT Workstation to NT Server 4.0 by using the WINNT32 command and installing NT 4.0 into the same directory that NT Workstation was installed to.

12. What will happen if you upgrade NT Server 3.51 to NT Server 4.0, and the 3.51 files were stored in \WINNT35 and the 4.0 files are stored in \WINNT?

_____

NT Server Roles

13.   The two server roles that maintain the domain SAM database are:

_____

_____

14.   The _____ server role maintains the read-write copy
of the domain SAM database.

15.   The _____ server role maintains the read-only copy of
the domain SAM database.

16.   What are the two main advantages of BDCs?

_____

_____

17.   List the three roles that an NT Server can play in an NT domain.

_____

_____

_____

18.   What is the advantage of installing an NT Server as a member server?

_____

19. True or False. A member server can be promoted to a BDC, but cannot be directly promoted to a PDC.

20. True or False. A BDC can be promoted to a PDC, but the PDC has to be up and running.

21. True or False. A BDC can become a part of another domain by selecting another domain through Control Panel ➤ Network and then providing an appropriate administrator account name and password.

22. True or False. A member server can become a part of another domain by selecting another domain through Control Panel ➤ Network and then providing an appropriate administrator account name and password.

23. True or False. If the PDC crashes, the first BDC that was installed will automatically be promoted to the PDC.

24. The _____ utility is used to promote a BDC to PDC.

25. You can have up to _____ PDC's in a domain.

26. True or False. You are required to have at least one BDC per domain.

27. True or False. The PDC does not have to be accessible during the installation of the BDC.

28. True or False. The PDC does not have to be available during the installation of a member server.

Installation Methods for NT Server

29.   True or False. During an express installation, you can choose the size and location of your paging file.

30.   You have 10 NT servers that need to be installed. You decide to use the over-the-network method. What is the name of the utility that is used to create the network startup disk?

_____

31.   In order to install NT Server over the network, what two preparation steps should be taken on the distribution server?

_____

_____

32.   True or False. You have 10 NT servers that you will be installing at the same time. You decide to use the over-the-network method. The same diskette can be used for all 10 computers.

33.   Which existing operating system clients can support NT Server installation using the over-the-network method?

_____

_____

_____

_____

_____

34. If you will be installing an Intel-based NT Server over the network, which sub-directory should be copied from the NT Server CD to the distribution server?

_____

35. True or False. In order to install NT Server onto an Intel computer, the computer must have an SCSI CD-ROM that is accessible through NT.

36. True or False. An Express installation will recognize and configure up to four network adapters that have been installed into your computer.

37. True or False. In order to configure a computer as a PDC, you must select a custom installation.

Configuring Protocols and Protocol Bindings

38. Which transport protocol requires the most configuration?

_____

39. Which transport protocol requires no configuration?

_____

40. If you were using NWLink on your network, and a client using NWLink was having connection problems, what would be the most likely configuration error?

_____

41. Which frame type does NWLink try to use if you use the Auto-detect feature?

_____

42. What is the default gateway option used for in TCP/IP configuration?

_____

43. What is the purpose of a DHCP server?

_____

44. What does DHCP stand for?

_____

45. Which command line utility can be used to view your IP configuration information?

_____

46. What three options should be configured if you are using manual IP configuration?

_____

_____

_____

47. In what two cases do you configure the NWLink internal network number?

_____

_____

48. What two options can be configured for NWLink IPX/SPX?

_____

_____

49. What is the term for the process that links the NDIS driver to the network protocol you are using?

_____

50. If you are using multiple network protocols, is their any significance in the order that the protocols are bound for each service, and if so, what is the significance?

_____

51. What is the subnet mask used for in TCP/IP configuration?

_____

52. True or False: If you are connecting to IPX/SPX resources that use both 802.2 and 802.3 frame types, you should select auto-detect frame configuration when configuring the NWLink protocol.

53. Which frame types can you use with NWLink if you are using Ethernet network adapter cards?

_____

_____

_____

_____

Configuring Network Adapters

54. Where do you configure network adapters in NT Server?

_____

55. What are four options that could potentially be configured on a network adapter?

_____

_____

_____

_____

56. What will happen if your software configuration in NT does not match your hardware configuration on your network adapter?

_____

57. Your computer will become a _____ if you configure it with two or more network adapters across two subnetworks.

58. True or False. If you install two network adapters in your NT server and are using TCP/IP, both adapters must be configured with the same IP address.

Configuring NT Server Core Services

59. Which computer(s) can act as an export computer if you are using directory replication?

_____

60. Which computer(s) can act as an import computer if you are using directory replication?

_____

61. Which two groups must the directory replicator service user account belong to?

_____

_____

62. Which computer(s) must run the directory replicator service: the export computer, the import computer, or both?

_____

63. Which utility is used to manage NT Server and client licenses?

_____

64. Which utility should be used to backup your server's registry?

_____

65. True or False. You can backup shared drives from the NT Backup program.

66. True or False. You can backup FAT or NTFS partitions from the NT Backup program.

67. Which two utilities can be used to define how NT services are configured?

_____

_____

68. What is the name of the default share that is used by the directory replicator import service?

_____

69. What is the default directory used by the export server in directory replication?

_____

70. What is the default directory used by the import server in directory replication?

_____

71.   What are the two licensing modes that NT supports?

_____

_____

72.   Which service should you use to copy read-only data, such as logon scripts and system policies, from one NT Server to another NT Server?

_____

73.   You use your NT Server as a workstation and support less than 10 incoming connections. Where do you configure the Minimize Memory Used option so that your server's performance will be optimized?

_____

74.   Your NT Server acts as a domain controller. Which server optimization choice should you use?

_____

75.   Your NT Server acts as an SQL server. Which server optimization choice should you use?

_____

Configuring Peripherals and Devices

76.   To configure peripherals, you use _____.

77. To configure network cards, you use Control Panel ➤ _____.

78. You have just installed a new SCSI adapter and a new tape drive. What two steps should you take?

_____

_____

79. You want to protect your server from power outages. You should install a _____ _____ and configure it through Control Panel ➤ _____ _____.

Configuring Hard Disks

80. Your computer has a drive that is used for the system and boot partition. In addition, you have four SCSI drives that are 1GB each. Which disk configuration will give you the most disk space for the SCSI drives?

_____

81. Your computer has a drive that is used for the system and boot partition. In addition, you have four SCSI drives that are 1GB each. Which disk configuration will give you the most disk space for the SCSI drives while also providing fault tolerance?

_____

82. What is the difference between disk mirroring and disk duplexing?

_____

83. NT has already been installed and has been running for a month. You have just added three new hard drives. The first drive has 300MB of hard disk space, the second 400MB of hard disk space, and the third with 50MB of hard disk space. Using the three new drives, you decide to implement a volume set. How much space is available for data?

_____

84. Would you use the scsi(0) or the multi(0) ARC naming convention with an IDE drive?

_____

85. Would you use the scsi(0) or the multi(0) ARC naming convention with an SCSI adapter with the BIOS enabled?

_____

86. Would you use the scsi(0) or the multi(0) ARC naming convention with an SCSI adapter with the BIOS disabled?

_____

87. True or False. The CONVERT command-line utility can be used to convert an NTFS partition to FAT.

88. NT has already been installed and has been running for a month. You have just added three new hard drives. The first drive has 300MB of hard disk space, the second 400MB of hard disk space, and the third with 500MB of hard disk space. Using the three new drives, you decide to implement a stripe set. How much space is available for data?

_____

89. The ARC naming conventions are used to point to the NT boot partition during startup in the _____ configuration file.

90. Your computer has two IDE drives. The first drive has one partition, which is logically defined as C:\. The second drive contains two partitions, which are D:\ and E:\. The system partition is on the C:\drive. The boot partition is on the E:\ drive. What is the correct ARC naming convention for this computer's NT boot partition?

_____

91. Your computer has one SCSI drive and the BIOS is enabled. There are two partitions on this drive. Both the system and the boot partition are on the first partition. What is the correct ARC naming convention for this computer?

_____

92. Your computer has one SCSI drive and the BIOS is disabled. There are two partitions on this drive. The system partition is on the first partition. The boot partition is on the second partition. What is the correct ARC naming convention for this computer?

_____

93. NT has already been installed and has been running for a month. You have just added three new hard drives. The first drive has 300MB of hard disk space, the second 400MB of hard disk space, and the third with 500MB of hard disk space. Using the three new drives, you decide to implement a stripe set with parity. How much space is available for data?

_____

94. The _____ command line utility is used to change a FAT partition to NTFS while still preserving the data.

95. The _____ hard disk configuration allows you to combine partitions of disk space that may or may not match in physical storage size.

Configuring Printers

96. True or False. The following clients can dynamically load their drivers from an NT Print Server.

a. _____ Windows 3.1

b. _____ Windows for Workgroups

c. _____ Windows 95

d. _____ Windows NT 3.1

e. _____ Windows NT 3.5/3.51

f. _____ Windows NT 4.0

97. What two conditions should be met before you implement a printer pool?

_____

_____

98. If you are connecting to an existing network printer, you should select (My Computer or Network Print Server) from the printer wizard.

99. The _____ tab within printer properties is used to setup a printing pool.

100. The _____ tab within printer properties is used to specify a printer's priority.

101. The _____ tab within printer properties is used to update an Intel Windows NT 4.0 print driver.

102. You have two groups of users that share the same physical print device. One group, the Managers, wants their print jobs to print before the other group, Sales. What should you do?

_____

103. What is the difference between the My computer and the Network print server option in the printer setup wizard?

_____

Configuring NT Server for Various Clients

104. True or False. Before you add an NT Workstation to a domain, you must create a computer account for the computer.

105. True or False. Before you add a Windows 95 computer to a domain, you must create a computer account for the computer.

106. Which utility is used to add computers to the domain?

_____

107. Where does an NT Workstation specify which domain they belong to?

_____

108. The _____ utility can be used to create the software that MS-DOS clients need to access the domain.

109. True or False. Windows 95 clients can be managed through Server Manager.

SAMPLE TEST

2-1   You are the head of the testing lab. You are currently configuring a computer that will boot between Windows 95, NT Workstation, and NT Server. You will have two hard drives and each hard drive will have a single partition. You want support for file names that exceed the DOS naming convention of 8.3. You also require that both partitions be accessible, no matter what operating system you boot to. Which file system is the best solution?

   A. FAT

   B. FAT32

   C. HPFS

   D. NTFS

2-2   You are installing five physical print devices for a secretarial pool. You want the users to be able to have their jobs go to the first available print device so you decide to implement a printer pool. What condition must be met first?

   A. All the printer devices must be the same make and model.

   B. All the print devices must use the same print driver.

   C. You must create a printer for each print device, then link them through the printer pool configuration tab.

   D. All of the printers must be network printers.

2-3   Your computer has an IDE drive that contains the system and boot partition. You are running out of disk space and add three new SCSI drives. The three drives consist of a 500MB drive and two 750MB drives. Because you are concerned with fault tolerance, you choose to use disk striping with parity. How much space can be used for data storage?

   A. 1,000MB

   B. 1,250MB

   C. 1,500MB

   D. 1,750MB

2-4 Your computer has an IDE drive that contains the system and boot partition. You are running out of disk space and add three new SCSI drives. The three drives consist of a 500MB drive and two 750MB drives. Because you are concerned with performance, you choose to use disk striping. How much space can be used for data storage?

    A. 1,000MB

    B. 1,250MB

    C. 1,500MB

    D. 1,750MB

2-5 Your computer has an IDE drive that contains the system and boot partition. You are running out of disk space and add three new SCSI drives. The three drives consist of a 500MB drive and two 750MB drives. Because you are concerned with disk space, you choose to use a volume set. How much space can be used for data storage?

    A. 1,000MB

    B. 1,250MB

    C. 1,500MB

    D. 2,000MB

2-6 Your computer has an IDE drive that contains the system and boot partition. You are running out of disk space and add three new SCSI drives. The three drives consist of a 500MB drive and two 750MB drives. Because you are concerned with fault tolerance, you choose to use disk striping with parity. How much space must be used for parity?

    A. 250MB

    B. 500MB

    C. 1,250MB

    D. 750MB

SAMPLE TEST

2-7 Your NT Server is configured as shown in the following diagram. The files needed to boot NT are on the C:\ drive and the \WINNT directory is on the D:\ drive. What is the correct ARC naming convention for this for this configuration?

    A. SCSI(0)DISK(0)RDISK(0)PARTITION(1)

    B. MULTI(0)DISK(0)RDISK(1)PARTITION(1)

    C. SCSI(0)DISK(1)RDISK(0)PARTITION(1)

    D. SCSI(0)DISK(0)RDISK(0)PARTITION(0)

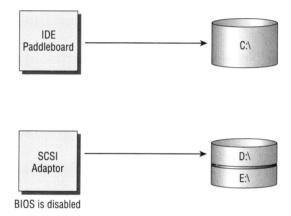

2-8 Your NT Server is configured as shown in the following diagram. The files needed to boot NT are on the C:\ drive and the \WINNT directory is on the F:\ drive. What is the correct ARC naming convention for this for this configuration?

    A. SCSI(0)DISK(1)RDISK(1)PARTITION(2)

    B. MULTI(1)DISK(0)RDISK(1)PARTITION(2)

    C. SCSI(1)DISK(1)RDISK(0)PARTITION(2)

    D. MULTI(1)DISK(1)RDISK(0)PARTITION(2)

2-9 At the end of the month the accounting department prints reports that are 300-500 pages in length. These reports are used for archival purposes. The accounting manager is complaining that when these reports are printed, the users have to wait for their short print jobs that are needed right away. What is the best solution for this problem?

A. Configure two printers named REPORTS and ACCT. Give the ACCT printer a higher priority than the REPORTS printer so that its jobs are always printed first.

B. Create two printers, REPORTS and ACCT. Configure the REPORTS printer to only be available after hours. Configure the REPORTS printer to be available 24 hours a day. Have users send the reports to the REPORTS printer.

C. Create two printers, REPORTS and ACCT. Configure the REPORTS printer to only print jobs after they have completely spooled. Specify that the ACCT printer should print jobs as soon as they start spooling.

D. Tell the user who prints the accounting reports to wait and submit the report job at the end of the day.

2-10 What is the name of the file that points to the NT boot partition through the ARC name?

    A. SYSTEM.INI

    B. BOOT.INI

    C. BOOT.CFG

    D. This information is provided through the registry.

2-11 In your test lab, you installed a computer as NT Server. The computer has one hard drive, with one partition that is defined as C:\. The partition is formatted with NTFS. You want to configure the computer so that it will also dual-boot Windows 95. What command will convert the partition to FAT, while still preserving the existing data?

    A. CONVERT C: /fs:FAT

    B. FORMAT C: /fs:FAT

    C. Use Disk Administrator to convert the partition to FAT.

    D. You can't complete this operation without losing the data and using a tape restore.

2-12 You installed NT Server with the /B switch and skipped the creation of the three startup disks. You now need to restore the ERD which requires you to use the three startup disks. You are currently running NT Server and you have access to the NT Server CD ROM. What command do you use?

    A. WINNT /ox

    B. WINNT32 /ox

    C. SETUP /disks

    D. WINNT /disks

SAMPLE TEST

2-13   In your test lab, you installed NT Server. You want to be able to use the features of NTFS, so you have decided to convert your D: drive to NTFS. You want to preserve your existing information. What is the easiest way to accomplish this task?

    A. Use Disk Administrator.

    B. Use Server Manager.

    C. Use FDISK.

    D. Use the CONVERT command line utility.

2-14   You are viewing the bindings order of the Workstation service. It lists the protocols in the following order:

NetBEUI

TCP/IP

NWLink

You are running Client Services for NetWare and are primarily communicating with a NetWare server using IPX/SPX. Based on this scenario, is there anything you can do to improve performance?

    A. You should leave the bindings as they are currently configured. Because NetBEUI has the lowest overhead, it should always go first.

    B. TCP/IP should be listed first, because it is the industry standard.

    C. NWLink should be moved to the top of the binding list, because it is your most commonly used protocol.

    D. Binding order has no impact on performance.

2-15 You have one PDC and two BDCs. You maintain the logon scripts and system policies file on the PDC. How should you manage this so that users who validate logons at the BDCs get their correct logon information?

    A. When specifying logon scripts and system policy files, use a UNC name that points to the PDC.

    B. Use the NT Explorer to copy the files from the PDC to the BDCs.

    C. Use the Directory Replicator service.

    D. Use the File Replicator service.

2-16 Your print server is running out of disk space. You add a new drive to the computer. Where do you configure the print server to use the alternate spooler location?

    A. Printer Properties ➤ Device Settings

    B. Printer Properties ➤ Printer Settings

    C. Printer Properties ➤ Spooler Settings

    D. The registry

2-17 You just received five new computers that need to have NT Server installed on them. You have decided to use the over-the-network method of installation. The new computers currently have no networking software installed. What two steps must you complete before you can complete your task? Choose all that apply.

    A. Copy the distribution files to a network server and create a share.

    B. Copy the distribution files and create a share through the Network Client Administrator.

    C. Create a network startup disk for each new computer through the Network Client Administrator.

    D. Create a network startup disk for each new computer through Server Manager.

2-18 On one of your test lab computers you installed Windows 95. You now want to upgrade the computer to NT Server and preserve your existing settings. The Windows 95 system files are in a directory called \WINDOWS. How should you proceed?

    A. Use the WINNT command and specify that NT Server should be installed into the \WINDOWS directory.

    B. Use the WINNT32 command and specify that NT Server should be installed into the \WINDOWS directory.

    C. Use the WINNT command with the /U switch and specify that NT Server use the \WINNT directory.

    D. Windows 95 has no upgrade path to NT Server.

2-19 You have decided to install NT Server onto a new computer. The new computer is currently only running DOS as an operating system. Which command should you use to install NT Server?

    A. SETUP.EXE

    B. WINNT.EXE

    C. WINNT32.EXE

    D. INSTALL.EXE

2-20 You installed NT Server with the /B switch and skipped the creation of the three startup disks. You now need to restore the ERD which requires you to use the three startup disks. You are currently sitting at a DOS machine that has the NT Server CD ROM. What command do you use?

    A. WINNT /ox

    B. WINNT32 /ox

    C. SETUP /disks

    D. WINNT /disks

2-21   On one of your test lab computers you installed NT Server 3.51. You now want to upgrade the computer to NT Server 4.0 and preserve your existing settings. The 3.51 boot partition is a directory called \WINNT35. How should you proceed?

    A. Use the WINNT command and specify that NT Server should be installed into the \WINNT directory.

    B. Use the WINNT32 command and specify that NT Server should be installed into the \WINNT35 directory.

    C. Use the WINNT command and specify that NT Server should be installed into the \WINNT35 directory.

    D. Use the WINNT command with the /U switch and specify that NT Server use the \WINNT directory.

2-22   You have a laser printer attached to your computer. Two of your co-workers also need to access your printer. You are concerned that other people in your department will also try and use your printer and want to limit their access. What two things should you do?

    A. Assign the Everyone group No Access to your printer.

    B. Remove the Everyone groups Print permission from your printer.

    C. Add your two co-workers to a group and grant their group Print permission to your printer.

    D. Disable the browser service on your computer, so your co-workers won't know that your printer has been shared.

2-23 You support a mixed client environment of DOS, Windows 3.*x*, Windows 95, and NT 3.51 Workstations, and NT 4.0 Workstations. You have a shared network printer. You want to provide dynamic drivers if possible. Which clients should you provide drivers for on the NT print server? Choose all that apply.

    A. DOS

    B. Windows 3.*x*

    C. Windows 95

    D. NT 3.51 Workstation

    E. NT 4.0 Workstation

2-24 You support 25 NT 4.0 Workstations. They attach to a Digital laser printer that is directly attached to the network. Digital has just released a new driver for the printer which offers significant enhancements over the previous driver. How do you update your clients?

    A. Copy the new driver onto a share and advise your users to update their driver.

    B. Update the driver on the print server, the next time the client restarts their computer and attaches to the printer they will automatically download the driver.

    C. Update the driver on the print server, the next time the client sends a job to the printer, the new driver will automatically update the client's old driver.

    D. Create a new printer and use the new driver. Let your users know they should send their print jobs to the new printer.

2-25 You are in a domain called CORP. Your PDC is called PDC and is configured to be an export computer. In the directory replication configuration box, you specify that the To List contains CORP. Who will the export computer(s) be? Choose all that apply.

    A. You can only add computer names in the To List, not domain names.

    B. Any member servers running the replicator service.

C. Any NT Workstations running the replicator service.

D. Any Windows 95 computers running the replicator service.

2-26   You have 50 workstations on your network. They are all using the NWLink IPX/SPX network protocol. Currently, half of the clients are configured to use the 802.3 frame type and the other half are configured to use the 802.2 frame type. You are installing a new server. How should you configure the server?

A. Use manual configuration and choose the 802.2 frame type.

B. Use manual configuration and choose the 802.3 frame type.

C. Use the auto-detect method for frame type.

D. Use manual configuration and choose 802.2 and 802.3 frame type.

2-27   Which utility is used to configure directory replication service?

A. Control Panel ➤ Services

B. Control Panel ➤ Directory Replicator

C. Service Manager

D. Server Manager

2-28   Your domain has a PDC and three BDCs. Your PDC currently acts as a PDC and also runs SQL. Your SQL server is performing very poorly. You decide that you want to dedicate the PDC to only acting as the SQL server. What do you do?

A. Promote one of the BDC's to PDC.

B. Demote the PDC to a BDC.

C. Demote the PDC to a member server.

D. Backup the PDC, re-install it as a member server, and restore the SQL server.

2-29 You have 100 new computers that you want to install Windows 95 on. You decide to use the over-the network installation. Which of the following steps should you take?

    A. Copy the Windows 95 distribution files to a network server.

    B. Create a share for the distribution files.

    C. Create a startup boot diskette using the Network Client Administrator.

    D. Boot using the startup floppy you created.

2-30 You are using TCP/IP in a non-routed network. What else besides the IP address must be configured?

    A. Default gateway

    B. Subnet mask

    C. DHCP server being used

    D. Nothing else is required except the IP address.

2-31 You are currently experiencing very high traffic on your LAN segment. What is the best solution to improve the situation?

    A. Install a second network adapter in your server and segment the traffic on two subnets.

    B. Specify that half your clients use the NWLink protocol and the other half use the TCP/IP protocol.

    C. Unbind unnecessary protocols.

    D. Disable any services that are not being used.

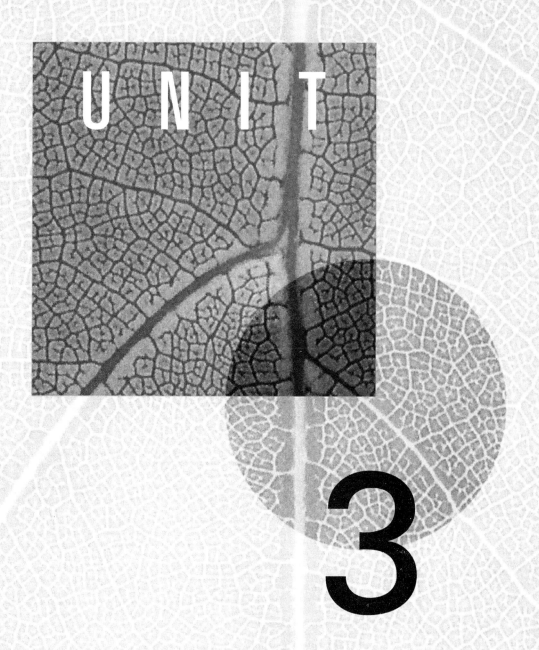

UNIT

3

Managing Resources

Test Objectives: Managing Resources

- **Manage users and group accounts. Considerations include:**
  - Managing Windows NT users
  - Managing Windows NT user rights
  - Managing Windows NT groups
  - Administering account policies
  - Auditing changes to the user account database

- **Create and manage policies and profiles for various situations. Policies and profiles include:**
  - Local user profiles
  - Roaming user profiles
  - System policies

- **Administer remote servers from various types of client computers. Client computer types include:**
  - Windows 95
  - Windows NT Workstation

- **Manage disk resources. Tasks include:**
  - Copying and moving files between file systems
  - Creating and sharing resources
  - Implementing permissions and security
  - Establishing file auditing

Exam objectives are subject to change at any time without prior notice and at Microsoft's sole discretion. Please visit Microsoft's Training & Certification website (www.microsoft.com/Train_Cert) for the most current exam objectives listing.

In the following sections, you will learn how to manage NT users and groups, profiles and system policies, remote administration, and disk resources.

User and Group Management

User and group management are common administrative tasks. This section will focus on how to manage NT users: user rights, NT groups, account policies, and how you can audit account management. All of these tasks will be accomplished through the User Manager for Domains utility.

Managing NT Users

To create and manage users, you use the User Manager for Domains utility. NT Server has only two default user accounts: Administrator and Guest (note the Guest account is disabled by default). This means you will probably have to create users.

In order to create and manage users, you must be logged on as a member of the Administrators or Account Operators group. The following subsections will cover creation and management of NT user accounts.

Creating User Accounts

Once you are in User Manager for Domains, you create a user by selecting User ➤ New User. You will see the New User dialog box (see Figure 3.1).

The options for creating a new user are shown in Table 3.1.

You can also specify user properties, which will be covered in the next subsection during user creation.

F I G U R E 3.1

The New User
dialog box

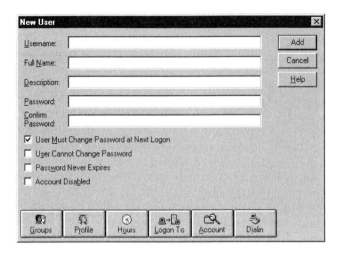

T A B L E 3.1

The New User Dialog
Box Configuration
Options

Option	Description
Username	A unique id used to identify the user. The username can be up to 20 characters and is typically a combination of alpha-numeric characters. The following characters are NOT allowed: " / \ [ ] ; : | = , + * ? < >. Username is the only required field for creation of a new user. It is actually a property of the User's Security ID (SID) and can be changed
Full Name	Designed to provide the user's first and last name, for informational purposes
Description	Can be used to provide further information for the user, such as title, department, or location
Password and Confirm Password	Specifies the users initial password
User Must Change Password at Next Logon	Checked by default. This option forces the user to change their password the first time they log on

T A B L E 3.1 *(cont.)*	Option	Description
The New User Dialog Box Configuration Options	User Cannot Change Password	Not specified by default. This option prevents a user from changing their password. This option is used for guest, service, and shared accounts
	Password Never Expires	This option allows you to override the password expiration in the Account Policy. This is typically used for guest and service accounts
	Account Disabled	Keeps an account from being accessed. This option is used for accounts that are not currently being used, but might be used again in the future and for template accounts

Managing User Accounts

Each user account has associated properties. These properties specify:

- Which groups the user belongs to
- Profile information
- The hours during the week when the user can log on
- Which computers the user account can log on from
- Account expiration and type

Groups   The Groups property defines what local and global groups the users belong to. Groups will be covered in more detail in the Managing NT Groups section.

If the user is logged on before they are added to a group, they must log off and log on again so that their access token will be updated with the group membership.

Profile   Specify many user options in the User Environment Profile dialog box (see Figure 3.2).

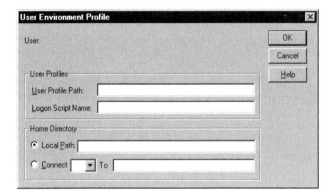

The options you can specify are listed in Table 3.2.

Option	Description
User Profile Path	This option is normally left blank, and indicates that the user will use a local profile. If the user will use a roaming profile, this box is filled in with a UNC path pointing to the location of the User Profiles, usually on PDC or BDC
Logon Script Name	Specifies a logon script that will run every time the user logs on. This is normally a .BAT or .EXE file. By default, NT will look for logon scripts in the NETLOGON share of the authenticating domain controller
Home Directory	Allows you to specify a home directory for the user. Home directories are normally used as a place for users to store their personal data files. You can specify that the home directory be on a local or network drive. The *%USERNAME%* variable can be used to substitute the users logon name

Hours   Logon hours are used to specify when a user is permitted to log on and access the network. By default, a user can log on 24 hours a day, seven days a week. You could limit this for:

- Security reasons
- Backup hours

Logon To   The Logon Workstations dialog box specifies which computers the user can log on to the domain from. By default, a user can log on from any client. Logon To can limit this up to eight clients, specified by Computer Name. For example, you might limit the Administrator account to only be able to log on from certain workstations within the domain for security purposes.

Account   The Account user property specifies two items:

- If the account has an expiration date, for example, for temporary employees.
- Whether the account is a global account or a local account.

Managing NT User Rights

User rights are used to specify the system tasks that users and groups have access to. User rights come in two flavors, regular user rights and advanced user rights. To specify user rights, you use User Manager for Domains, Policies ➤ User Rights. The regular user rights are defined in Table 3.3.

	User Right	Description	Default Membership
T A B L E 3.3 NT User Rights defined	Access this computer from the network	Allows a user to connect to this computer from another network location	Administrators, Everyone
	Add workstations to the domain	Allows a user to add NT computers to the domain	Account Operators, Administrators
	Backup files and directories	Overrides any permissions to allow a user to back up the file system	Administrators, Server Operators, Backup Operators
	Change the system time	Used to change the computer's internal system time	Administrators, Server Operators

	User Right	Description	Default Membership
T A B L E 3.3 *(cont.)* NT User Rights defined	Force shutdown from a remote system	Not currently implemented	Administrators, Server Operators
	Load and unload device drivers	Used to load and unload device drivers dynamically	Administrators
	Log on locally	Allows the user to log on at the local computer. Normally users do not log on at NT servers; they log on to the domain through network clients	Account Operators, Administrators, Backup Operators, Print Operators, Server Operators
	Manage auditing and security log	Used to view audit log files if auditing has been enabled	Administrators
	Restore files and directories	Overrides any permissions to allow a user to restore the file system	Administrators, Server Operators, Backup Operators
	Shut down the system	Allows users to shut down the computer	Account Operators, Administrators, Backup Operators, Print Operators, Server Operators
	Take ownership of files or other objects	Allows a user to take ownership of an NTFS file or folder or other object, such as a printer	Administrators

Managing NT Groups

Normally you assign user rights and permissions to a group as opposed to an individual user. It is much easier for an administrator to manage and troubleshoot group permissions as opposed to individual users.

NT supports two types of groups: local groups and global groups.

Local Groups

Local groups have the following characteristics:

- The purpose of a local group is to assign resource permissions to a single entity of users and Global Groups.

- Local groups can be created on any NT computer.

- When you create a local group, it resides in the NT computer's local SAM database.

- Local groups can contain:

  - Users from the local SAM database

  - Users from within the domain

  - Users from trusted domains

  - Global groups from within the domain

  - Global groups from trusted domains

Global Groups

Global groups have the following characteristics:

- The purpose of a global group is to logically group users who have similar network requirements.

- Global groups can only reside on NT domain controllers.

- Global groups can only contain users from within the local domain.

Local Group and Global Group Interaction

Local groups and global groups are designed to work as follows:

1. At the NT computer that contains a shared network resource, you create a local group and assign the access permissions the local group will require.

2. From a domain controller (or computer with administrative tools), create a global group that contains the users who need to access the resource.

3. At the NT computer that contains the shared network resource, add the global group from step 2 to the local group created in step 1.

For example (see Figure 3.3), Rick, Kevin, and Katie are all users within your domain who need to access the EMAIL share on the member server APPS. You should manage the groups as shown:

FIGURE 3.3

Group interaction example

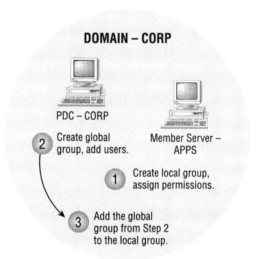

In this example, you would manage NT groups by:

1. Creating a local group called Email Users on the member server APPS. Assign the access rights that users will need for the EMAIL resource.

2. Create a global group called Domain Email on the PDC, CORP. Add the users Rick, Kevin, and Katie.

3. Add the global group Domain Email to the local group Email Users.

Administering Account Policies

Account policies are used to specify password and account restrictions. To access the Account Policy dialog box (see Figure 3.4), you select Policies ➤ Account in the main window of User Manager for Domains. These options are defined in Table 3.4 and Table 3.5.

FIGURE 3.4

The Account Policy
dialog box

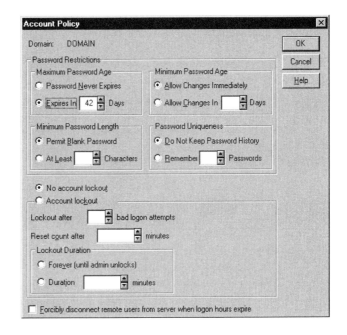

T A B L E 3.4: Password Restrictions

Password Restriction	Description	Values	Default Value
Maximum Password Age	Maximum number of days a password can be valid	1-999	42 days
Minimum Password Age	Minimum number of days a password can be valid	1-999	Allow changes immediately
Minimum Password Length	Specifies if a password is required or not, and if a password is required, how many characters it must be	1-14	Allow changes immediately
Password Uniqueness	Specifies how many unique passwords must be used before a user can re-use a password	1-24	Do not keep password history

T A B L E 3.5: Account Restrictions

Account Restrictions	Description	Values	Default Value
No account lockout or Account lockout	Specifies whether account lockout should be enabled or not	This is set or not set; the following options assume account lockout is enabled	No account lockout
Lockout after	Specifies how many attempts a user can make when trying to log on	1-999	If account lock-out is enabled, 5
Reset count after	Specifies how many minutes between failed logon attempts before account is reset	1-99,999 minutes	If account lock-out is enabled, 30
Lockout duration	Specifies how long an account should be locked if the account lockout restrictions are exceeded. Can specify forever (administrator must unlock) or a set duration in minutes	1-99,999 minutes	If account lock-out is enabled, 30

Auditing Accounts Management

You can audit changes made to the accounts database by using User Manager for Domains, then accessing Policies ≻ Audit. To enable auditing, you click on Audit These Events in the Audit Policy dialog box (see Figure 3.5).

F I G U R E 3.5

The Audit Policy dialog box

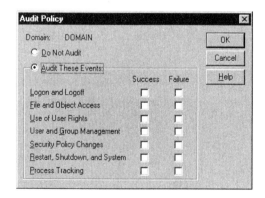

Once auditing is enabled, you can choose what success events, failure events, or both, you want to manage. Audit options include:

- Logon and Logoff
- File and Object Access
- User of User Rights
- User and Group Management
- Security Policy Changes
- Restart, Shutdown, and System
- Process Tracking

To view the results of your audit, you use Event Viewer and select the Security log.

Profiles and System Polices

Profiles and system polices are used to manage NT user and workstation configurations.

A profile is used to configure user settings such as desktop appearance, program groups, shortcuts, and network connections. Profiles come in different flavors, local or roaming, and you can make them read-only by imposing mandatory profiles.

System policies configure the user environment and what actions the user can perform. System policies can be applied to users, groups, and specific computers. System policies are implemented by making changes to the registry with the System Policy Editor.

Local User Profiles

By default, NT uses a local profile. When a user logs on for the first time, a profile is created on the local NT computer in a directory called \WINNT\PROFILES in a subdirectory that matches the user's login name. For example, Katie's profile would be stored in \WINNT\PROFILES\KATIE. This works well if you only log on in one location. To use or access a user's profile from any network client, you must use a roaming profile.

Roaming User Profiles

Roaming profiles make a profile accessible over the network. This is especially useful for users who may have more than one workstation or who move around.

To create a roaming profile, complete the following steps:

1. Create a network share in a folder on a domain controller that contains the user profile.

2. In the User Environment Profile dialog box (Figure 3.2), specify the UNC path to the directory that contains the roaming profile.

Mandatory User Profiles

By default, profiles are read-write. The actual profile file is called NTUSER.DAT. It is possible that you do not want users to change their profiles. This could be for control purposes or because the profile is shared by a group of users. In this case, you can specify that the profile is mandatory by renaming NTUSER.DAT to NTUSER.MAN.

Remember, if a mandatory profile is unavailable (for example, if the server that stores the profile goes down), then the user will not be able to log on successfully.

System Policies

System policies are used to configure the user's environment. They are configured through the System Policy Editor. System policies work by editing the registry to reflect whatever settings you have imposed. System policies can be applied to:

- Users

- Groups

- Computers

System policies should reside in the \WINNT\SYSTEM32\REPL\IMPORT directory, which is the NETLOGON share. NT system policies are named NTCONFIG.POL.

Remote Administration

Remote administration makes it possible to administer an NT domain from a Windows 95 client or a Windows NT Workstation client. These administration tools can be installed from the NT Server distribution CD.

Windows 95

A Windows 95 computer that installs the NT administrative tools can access the following utilities:

- User Manager for Domains
- Server Manager
- Event Viewer

NT Workstation

An NT Workstation that installs the NT administrative tools gets a much wider selection of administrative tools. They include:

- User Manager for Domains
- Server Manager
- Event Viewer
- DHCP Manager
- WINS Manager
- System Policy Editor
- Services for Macintosh Editor
- Remote Access Administrator
- Remoteboot Manager

Main Remote Administration Utilities

The main administrative utilities that are used are:

- User Manager for Domains
- Server Manager

The User Manager for Domains utility has already been covered. The Server Manager utility is also used for remote management. This is a very powerful tool that allows you to:

- Manage computers' properties remotely
- Manage shares on remote computers
- Manage services on remote computers

In addition, when you install the remote administration tools on Windows 95 or Windows NT Workstations, the schema of Explorer and My Computer are extended to allow you to support and manage remote NTFS security and network printers.

Disk Resource Management

In this section, you will learn about disk resource management through copying and moving files, creating and sharing resources, permissions and security, and file auditing.

Copying and Moving Files

The difference between a copy and a move is:

- A copy will copy the file, so that it remains in the source and also exists at the destination.
- A move will move the file from the source to the destination.

This section will cover what will happen to file attributes and permissions, based on different actions you can take.

NTFS to NTFS

You can copy and move within the same NTFS partition or between different NTFS partitions. This will determine what attributes and permissions the files will have.

Same NTFS Partition   Assume that you are copying and moving files between the same NTFS partition, for example, from D:\DATA to D:\DOCS; you can expect the following:

- Copied files will inherit the same permissions and attributes as the destination directory.

- Moved files will keep the permissions and attributes from the source directory.

Different NTFS Partitions   On the other hand, if you are copying and moving files between different NTFS partitions, you will notice different results. For example, if your source directory was D:\DOCS and your destination directory was E:\DOCS, you could expect the following:

- Both copied and moved files would receive the permissions of the destination directory.

NTFS and FAT

If you were copying and moving files between NTFS and FAT, this becomes less relevant because FAT does not support permissions like NTFS does.

- Going from NTFS to FAT, you lose all permissions.

- Going from FAT to NTFS, your files will have the same permissions as the destination NTFS folder.

Creating and Sharing Resources

It is possible to create and share resources on FAT and NTFS partitions. In order to create a network share, you must be logged on as a member of the Administrators or Server Operators groups.

You can create shares through the NT Explorer, My Computer, WinFile (File Manager), and Server Manager.

Here, we'll assume that we're using NT Explorer. To create a share, click on the folder you want to share, then go to File ➤ Sharing. You will see the Sharing tab page (see Figure 3.6).

From the main dialog box, you can configure the options shown in Table 3.6.

FIGURE 3.6

The Sharing tab page

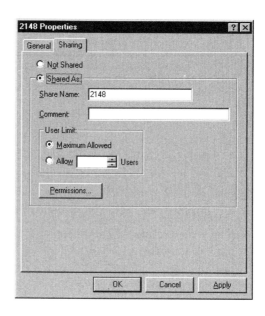

TABLE 3.6

Sharing Dialog Box
Options

Option	Description
Not Shared or Shared As	Specifies whether or not the folder can be shared. If the folder is shared, the other configuration options can be applied
Share Name	Name users will see when browsing through utilities like Network Neighborhood
Comment	Allows an optional informational comment
User Limit	Allows you to specify if the share should be limited, and if so, how many users can access the share concurrently
Permissions	These are covered in Table 3.7

In addition, you can specify which permissions will apply for users and groups to the share. By default, the share permissions allow Full Control to the Everyone group, but you can limit this by manipulating permissions in the Access Through Share Permissions dialog box (see Figure 3.7).

FIGURE 3.7

The Access Through
Share Permissions
dialog box

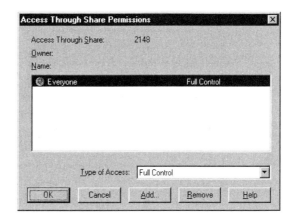

The permissions are defined in Table 3.7.

TABLE 3.7	**Share Permission**	**Description**
Share permissions defined	No Access	No Access means that you do not have access to the shared folder. Even if you have other permissions through your user or group memberships, you will not be able to access the share, because No Access overrides all other permissions
	Read	Read can be used to view files and folders, view data, and run programs
	Change	With Change, you incorporate Read with the ability to add files and folders, edit data, and delete files and folders
	Full Control	This is the whole enchilada. With Full Control you get everything that Read and Change offer with the ability change share permissions

With the exception of No Access, your access permissions will be cumulative, meaning you will receive the highest level of access that has been granted through your user account or group memberships.

Permissions and Security

In this section, permissions refer to file level (also called local) security that can be applied to NTFS files and folders. Local security is more detailed than share permissions and allows very specific control over file resources.

Local security applies to users who are logged in locally to a computer and users who access the same resource over the network. In the case that local and share security have been applied, the more restrictive permissions will be enforced.

To apply local security, you can use NT Explorer, My Computer, and Win-File (File Manager). In this case, we'll assume you are using NT Explorer. To assign local security, you would take the following steps:

1. Within NT Explorer, single click the file or folder you want to apply permissions to.

2. Go to File ➤ Properties.

3. Click on the Security tab.

4. Click the Permissions option to see the Directory Permissions dialog box (see Figure 3.8).

F I G U R E   3.8

The Directory Permissions dialog box

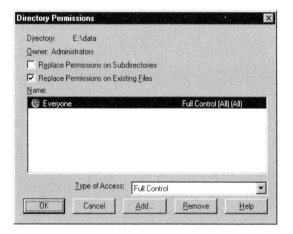

The default permissions are that group Everyone has Full Control. You can modify this for whatever is appropriate for your environment. The default permissions assignments are:

- Permissions are not replaced on subdirectories.

- Permissions are replaced on files within the parent directory.

The local or NTFS permissions are defined in Table 3.8.

	Permission	Description	Applies to Folder	Applies to File
T A B L E 3.8 Local NTFS Permissions defined	No Access	User has no rights to the specified resource. This right overrides any other rights the user may have through the user account or through group memberships	✓	✓
	List	Displays a listing of files and folders within the current directory, also allows you to change to subdirectories	✓	
	Read	Allows you to read files and execute programs, and list permissions above	✓	✓
	Add	Used to only add files and directories to the specified directory	✓	
	Add and Read	Just like it sounds, combines the permissions of Add and Read	✓	
	Change	Gives you the combined permissions of List, Add, and Read. In addition, you can edit files and delete data within a folder or file	✓	✓

T A B L E 3.8 *(cont.)* Local NTFS Permissions defined	Permission	Description	Applies to Folder	Applies to File
	Full Control	Gives you the combined permissions of all other rights. In addition, you can take ownership of files and directories	✓	✓
	Special Directory Access	Used to customize access permissions for folders. You can choose from Read, Write, Execute, Delete, Change Permissions, and Take Ownership	✓	
	Special File Access	Used to customize access permissions for files. You can choose from Read, Write, Execute, Delete, Change Permissions, and Take Ownership		✓

File Auditing

You can audit file events on NTFS partitions. In order to enable file auditing, you must first enable auditing of File and Object Access through User Manager for Domains ➤ Policies ➤ Audit. Once this is completed, you can configure file auditing through NT Explorer, My Computer, or WinFile (File Manager).

To enable and configure auditing, you would complete the following steps:

1. Use NT Explorer and single-click on the file or folder you wish to audit.

2. Select File ➤ Properties ➤ Security tab.

3. You will see the Directory Auditing dialog box (see Figure 3.9). From this box, specify which users or groups you wish to audit and which events you wish to track.

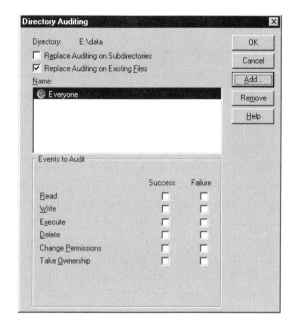

The Directory Auditing
dialog box

The options you can audit are:

- Read

- Write

- Execute

- Delete

- Change Permissions

- Take Ownership

Once you have enabled auditing, you can view the results through the
Security log within Event Viewer.

User and Group Management

1.   The _____ utility is used to create and manage NT users.

2.   What is the best way to prevent an NT account that is not currently being used (but will be used in the future) from posing a security risk?

_____

3.   What is the variable that can be used with logon scripts and home directories to substitute a users logon name with the variable?

_____

4.   True or False. NT User rights are used to specify what access a user has to an NTFS folder or file.

5.   What user rights grant a user or group the right to perform NT back and restore operations?

_____

6.   What does the Log On Locally user right allow?

_____

7.   By default, who has the user right Take Ownership Of Files Or Other Objects?

_____

8. To define NT user rights, you use User Manager for Domains ➤ _____

_____.

9. The main purpose of the _____ group is to logically group domain users together.

10. What users or groups can a global group contain?

_____

11. What is the main purpose of setting account lockout?

_____

12. Which restriction defines if a password can be used again or not?

_____

13. Which utility is used to view the results of auditing of the accounts database?

_____

14. The main purpose of a _____ group is to assign access permissions to resources that are controlled by a workstation.

15. What are the two default users that are created for NT domains?

_____

_____

16. The _____ option can be configured for a user account so that they do not have to change their password. This option will override the system password expiration policy.

17. What users and groups can a local group contain?

_____

18. If you specify a user logon script, what share will NT look in on the authenticating domain controller?

_____

19. Which group(s) can view the auditing files by default?

_____

20. You are concerned about your server's integrity. How do you specify that only members of the Administrators group should be able to shut the server down?

_____

21. Which groups can change the system time by default?

_____

22. Where do global groups reside?

_____

23. Where do local groups reside?

_____

24. To manage local and global groups, you would complete the following steps:

At an NT computer, create a _____ group and assign resource permissions to this group.

At the PDC, create a _____ group and add users.

Add the _____ group to the _____ _____ group at the computer which controls the resource.

25. NT users can have passwords up to _____ characters in length.

26. What happens if you configure the lockout duration forever and account lockout is imposed on a user account?

_____

27. To view the results of account database auditing, you would look at the _____ _____ log in Event Viewer.

28. Which user or group(s) can enable account database auditing?

_____

29. If you wanted to restrict a user account to only log on from specific workstations, what would you do?

_____

30. Which audit option would you choose if you wanted to track successful creation of new users and groups?

_____

31. Who can create and manage NT users and groups by default?

_____

32. If a user is logged on and the administrator adds the user to a new group, what does the user need to do so that they will have access to the resources that the new group has permissions to?

_____

Profiles and Polices

33. What is the default location for user profiles?

_____

34. By default, does NT use local profiles or roaming profiles?

_____

35. NT look for system policy files in the_____ folder.

36. What do you do to create mandatory user profiles?

_____

37. System policies are set by making changes to the _____.

38. System policies can be created for:

_____

_____

_____

39. By default, your profile is named _____.

40. NT system policies are stored in a file called _____.

41. Which utility is used to specify that a user is using a roaming profile?

_____

42. Which utility is used to create and manage system policies?

_____

Remote Administration

43. Which three administrative tools can be run from a Windows 95 client?

_____

_____

_____

44. When you install the administrative tools on a client, what utilities have their schema extended to support operations such as remote NTFS administration and network printer administration?

_____

_____

45. If you wanted to create a remote share on an NT workstation, which utility would you use?

_____

46.   Which utility is used to manage services on remote NT workstations?

_____

47.   True or False. An NT Workstation that is running the remote administrative tools can use the DHCP Manager to manage remote computers.

48.   True or False. An NT Workstation that is running the remote administrative tools can use the Disk Administrator to manage remote computers.

49.   Which client types can perform remote NT administration from the tools provided on the NT Server 4.0 CD?

_____

_____

Disk Resource Management

50.   List the four share permissions.

_____

_____

_____

_____

51.   True or False. Share permissions can be applied to files and folders.

52.   Rick is a member of the Engineers and Managers groups. What would Rick's effective permissions be on an NTFS folder that had the following permission applied?

Engineers   Read

Managers   Change

53.   Ron is a member of the Engineers and Managers groups. What would Rick's effective permissions be on an NTFS folder that had the following permission applied?

Engineers   No Access

Managers   Full Control

54.   What happens to NTFS permissions if you move a file from one NTFS partition to another NTFS partition?

55.   What happens to NTFS permissions if you move a file from one NTFS partition to another folder on the same NTFS partition?

56. What happens to NTFS permissions if you copy a file from one NTFS partition to another NTFS partition?

57. What happens to NTFS permissions if you copy a file from one NTFS partition to another folder on the same NTFS partition?

58. True or False. Local NTFS permissions can be applied to files and folders.

59. True or False. You can perform file auditing on FAT and NTFS partitions.

60. Once you have generated activity from a file audit, which utility do you use to view the audit log?

61. What is the minimum share permission that you can apply and still allow a user to edit data and delete files?

62. What are the default NTFS permissions assigned?

S T U D Y   Q U E S T I O N S

63. What are the default share permissions when a new share is created?

_____

64. Which NTFS folder permission allows you to customize access rights?

_____

65. Which option must be set in Auditing Policies in User Manager for Domains before file auditing can be enabled?

_____

66. True or False. When you apply NTFS permissions to a folder, those permissions are also applied to sub-folders by default.

67. True or False. When you apply NTFS permissions to a folder, those permissions are also applied to any files within the folder by default.

68. True or False. A user that has the NTFS Full Control permission can specify NTFS permissions for other users and groups on the folder for which he has Full Control permission to.

69. What groups have the ability to create and manage network shares?

_____

_____

SAMPLE TEST

3-1 You are the administrator for an NT domain. You are having problems with your backups because your users are not logging out properly at the end of the day and files are being left open. What is the best way to manage this situation?

A. Configure the account policy in User Manager for Domains so that users are not able to log on during unauthorized hours.

B. Configure each user account in User Manager for Domains so that users are unable to log on during unauthorized hours.

C. Create a user template that limits logon hours and copy all new users using this template.

D. Use Server Manager to specify what the allowable logon hours for the domain are.

3-2 One of your users, Fred, thinks he's General Hacker. You suspect that he is trying to break into users' accounts by trying obvious passwords. What two steps should you take?

A. Cut off his fingers.

B. Configure auditing for logon success.

C. Configure auditing for logon failure.

D. Configure account lockout in User Manager for Domains.

E. Configure intruder detection in User Manager for Domains.

3-3 What will happen if you copy a file between the same NTFS partition?

A. The file will inherit the NTFS permissions at the destination directory.

B. The file will retain the NTFS permissions from the source directory.

C. The file will default to the default NTFS permissions.

D. It will depend on which utility was used to copy the file.

SAMPLE TEST

3-4   What will happen if you move a file between the same NTFS partition?

    A. The file will inherit the NTFS permissions at the destination directory.

    B. The file will retain the NTFS permissions from the source directory.

    C. The file will default to the default NTFS permissions.

    D. It will depend on which utility was used to copy the file.

3-5   What will happen if you move a file from one NTFS partition to another NTFS partition?

    A. The file will inherit the NTFS permissions at the destination directory.

    B. The file will retain the NTFS permissions from the source directory.

    C. The file will default to the default NTFS permissions.

    D. It will depend on which utility was used to copy the file.

3-6   One of your users frequently moves from one NT workstation to another. He is complaining that whenever he logs on, he gets a different profile. Where can you specify that the users should have a roaming profile?

    A. Control Panel ➤ Network

    B. Control Panel ➤ System ➤ User Profile tab

    C. Server Manager

    D. User Manager for Domains

3-7   You are creating a template user for the accounting group. Your domain is called NTDO-MAIN, and you have created a share called USERS on a member server called ACCT. What should you specify in the path for the user's home directory?

    A. \\NTDOMAIN\ACCT\USERS\%LOGONNAME%

    B. \\NTDOMAIN\ACCT\USERS\%USERNAME%

C. \\ACCT\USERS\%LOGONNAME%

D. \\ACCT\USERS\%USERNAME%

3-8   You have just realized that the time is set incorrectly on your NT Server. By default, which groups can change the system time?

A. Account Operators

B. System Operators

C. Server Operators

D. Backup Operators

E. Administrators

3-9   Which utility is used to enable auditing of File and Object Access?

A. NT Explorer

B. My Computer

C. Server Manager

D. User Manager for Domains

3-10   Which utility would be used to manage network printers from a Windows 95 client that has had the NT administration tools installed?

A. NT Explorer

B. My Computer

C. Server Manager

D. User Manager for Domains

3-11   You are trying to create a network share on an NT domain controller, but the sharing tab is not showing up. What group(s) would you have to be a member of in order to be able to create a network share?

    A. Administrators

    B. Power Users

    C. Account Operators

    D. Server Operators

3-12   You have just hired a new user, Ron, who will be responsible for managing all temporary employees. You want Ron to be able to create and manage the temporary employees' user accounts within the domain. What is the minimum assignment that must be made for Ron?

    A. Grant Ron the Create And Manage Users And Groups user right.

    B. Make Ron a member of the Account Operators group.

    C. Make Ron a member of the Power Users group.

    D. Make Ron a member of the Server Operators group.

3-13   Your domain is called CORP. You have a PDC called CORPPDC. You also have a member server called SALES. You have 30 people in the Sales department who need to access the data on the SALES server. What two steps do you take before linking the local group and global groups together?

    A. Create a global group on the SALES server, assign permissions to this new global group.

    B. Create a local group on the SALES server, assign permissions to this new local group.

    C. Create a local group on CORPPDC, add users.

    D. Create a global group on CORPPDC, add users.

3-14 You have just created a local group on your NT member server, APPS. Which of the following users and groups can belong to your new local group?

    A. Users from your domain

    B. Local groups from your domain

    C. Global groups from your domain

    D. Users from trusting domains

    E. Users from trusted domains

3-15 You have just created a global group on your NT member server, APPS. Which of the following users and groups can belong to your new global group?

    A. Users from your domain

    B. Local groups from your domain

    C. Global groups from your domain

    D. Users from trusting domains

    E. Users from trusted domains

3-16 You have just spent days specifying and configuring the profile that will be used by the sales users. The users all share a common profile, and you need to configure it so that one user does not change the profile and affect the profile for all users. What step should you take?

    A. Rename the `NTUSER.DAT` file to `NTUSER.MAN`.

    B. In the System Profile Editor, check the mandatory profile radio button.

    C. Specify that the profile is mandatory in Control Panel ➢ System ➢ Profiles.

    D. Specify that the profile is mandatory through the System Policy Editor.

SAMPLE TEST

3-17 You have just configured the system policies for your domain. What location and file name should you specify?

    A. \WINNT\POLICIES\NTUSER.DAT

    B. \WINNT\POLICES\NTCONFIG.POL

    C. \WINNT\SYSTEM32\REPL\IMPORT\SCRIPTS\NTUSER.DAT

    D. \WINNT\SYSTEM32\REPL\IMPORT\SCRIPTS\NTCONFIG.POL

3-18 Which utility would be used to manage remote NTFS permissions from a Windows 95 client that has had the NT administration tools installed?

    A. NT Explorer

    B. My Computer

    C. Server Manager

    D. User Manager for Domains

3-19 Which utility would be used to create a remote share on an NT computer on a Windows 95 client that has had the NT administration tools installed?

    A. NT Explorer

    B. My Computer

    C. Server Manager

    D. User Manager for Domains

3-20 You recently added Terry to the Administrators group. However, when she tries to access resources that the Administrators group has rights to, she is denied. What is the most likely problem?

    A. Terry needs to log out and log on again to update her access token.

    B. Terry needs to change her password before she can use the new group membership.

C. Terry's account was probably disabled by accident.

D. You should double check and make sure the Administrators group has rights to the resources that Terry is trying to access.

3-21   You have decided to implement logon scripts. You create the scripts, but are not sure where the scripts should be stored. You ask the resident NT guru. Where does she tell you to place the scripts?

A. In the SCRIPTS share

B. In the NETLOGON share

C. In the IPC$ share

D. In the NETLOGON$ share

3-22   Which of the following are not account policies?

A. Allowed logon hours

B. Password restriction

C. Allowed logon workstations

D. Account lockout features

3-23   You have configured no profile information. When Michelle logs on to the domain from her NT workstation, where will her profile be stored by default?

A. On the authenticating domain controllers \WINNT\PROFILES\MICHELLE folder

B. On the Michelle's workstation's \WINNT\PROFILES\MICHELLE folder

C. On the authenticating domain controllers \WINNT\SYSTEM32\REPL\IMPORT\ PROFILES\MICHELLE folder

D. On the Michelle's workstation's \WINNT\SYSTEM32\REPL\IMPORT\PROFILES\ MICHELLE folder

---

SAMPLE TEST

3-24 You are creating a system policy that you want to enforce in your domain. What should you call the system policy file, and where should it be stored?

    A. \WINNT\POLICIES\CONFIG.NT

    B. \WINNT\POLICIES\NTCONFIG.POL

    C. \WINNT\SYSTEM32\REPL\IMPORT\SCRIPTS\CONFIG.NT

    D. \WINNT\SYSTEM32\REPL\IMPORT\SCRIPTS\NTCONFIG.POL

3-25 You have an application that is licensed for 20 users. How can you enforce this license through NT?

    A. Use the License Manager utility.

    B. Store the application in an NTFS folder, and apply a user limit.

    C. When you share the folder that the application is stored in, specify a user limit.

    D. NT has no mechanism to limit user access to applications.

UNIT

4

Connectivity

Test Objectives: Connectivity

- Configure Windows NT Server for interoperability with NetWare servers by using various tools. Tools include:
  - Gateway Services for NetWare
  - Migration Tool for NetWare

- Install and configure Remote Access Server (RAS). Configuration options include:
  - Configuring RAS communications
  - Configuring RAS protocols
  - Configuring RAS security
  - Configuring Dial-Up Networking clients

 Exam objectives are subject to change at any time without prior notice and at Microsoft's sole discretion. Please visit Microsoft's Training & Certification website (www.microsoft.com/Train_Cert) for the most current exam objectives listing.

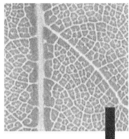

In this unit, you will learn about NetWare and RAS connectivity.

NetWare Connectivity

One of NT's greatest strengths is the ability to exist in a heterogeneous network environment. To support mixed networks of NT and NetWare, NT ships with Gateway Services for NetWare (GSNW). In order to ease shifts from existing NetWare servers to NT Servers, Microsoft includes the Migration Tool for NetWare utility.

To help alleviate confusion, Table 4.1 provides an overview of the protocol and services that are related to NetWare connectivity.

T A B L E 4.1: Overview of NetWare Connectivity Protocols and Services

Protocol or Service	Platform	Main Features	Benefits	Drawbacks
NWLink IPX/SPX Compatible Transport	Any NT Platform	This is an easily configured, routable protocol. Used by itself, it provides access to other servers running NetBIOS applications	Used to support CSNW, GSNW, and Migration Tool for NetWare	By itself, it provides no access for NT users trying to access NetWare resources or NetWare users trying to access NT resources

T A B L E 4.1:   Overview of NetWare Connectivity Protocols and Services **_(Continued)_**

Protocol or Service	Platform	Main Features	Benefits	Drawbacks
Client Services for NetWare (CSNW)	Only installed in NT Workstations	Allows an NT user to access NetWare file and print resources	Provides better performance than GSNW	Requires a user account and license on the NetWare server and takes up resources on the NT Workstation
Gateway Services for NetWare (GSNW)	Only installed on NT servers	Allows clients attached to the NT server to access NetWare file and print resources	Only one user connection is used on the NetWare server and no additional software is required on client computers	GSNW provides slower access to clients who are going through the gateway as opposed to using a NetWare redirector on their client computers
File and Print Services for NetWare	NT servers	Allows the NT server to emulate a NetWare server so that NetWare users can access NT file and print resources	NetWare users can access NT file and print resources	Does not ship with NT and you have to purchase it separately

Gateway Services for NetWare

Gateway Service for NetWare (GSNW) provides access to NetWare file and print resources for users who are logged in locally at the NT server or clients that are attached to the NT server (see Figure 4.1).

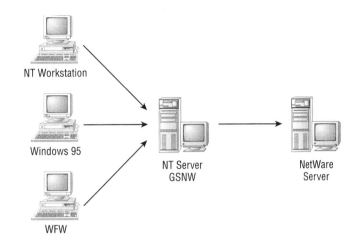

FIGURE 4.1

GSNW access

NT Workstation

Windows 95

WFW

NT Server
GSNW

NetWare
Server

Benefits of GSNW

- Clients attached to the NT server running GSNW that are using the Microsoft client software can access NetWare file and print resources.

- Users logged in locally at the NT server can access NetWare file and print resources.

- The GSNW connection only takes up one NetWare license, regardless of the number of users using the gateway.

Drawbacks of GSNW

- GSNW provides a slower connection than CSNW. Performance will be dependent on the number of users connected to the NetWare server.

- All users who access the Gateway will have the same permissions on the NetWare server.

Pre-Requisites for Installing GSNW

GSNW can only be installed onto NT servers. Before GSNW can be installed, the following pre-requisites should be met.

Pre-Requisites for the NT Server   The NT server must be running the NWLink IPX/SPX Compatible Transport protocol.

Pre-Requisites for the NetWare Server   The NetWare server requires the following setup:

- A user account should be created that has been assigned access permissions to the resources that the NT gateway users will need to access.

- A NetWare group named needs to be created on the server that you will connect to NTGATEWAY.

- The user you created for the gateway users must be added to the NTGATEWAY group.

You can assign the permissions to resources that gateway users need access to through the NetWare user or the NTGATEWAY group.

Installing and Configuring GSNW

To install GSNW, access Control Panel ➤ Network ➤ Services tab. Once you are in the Services dialog screen, click the Add button and select Gateway (and client) Services for NetWare. After you specify the location of the distribution files and install the required files, you must restart your computer. If not installed previously, the NWLink SPX/IPX network protocol will also be installed.

Once GSNW has been installed, you will see a new icon in Control Panel for GSNW. This icon is used to configure GSNW. GSNW is configured two ways: basic configuration and the gateway configuration.

GSNW Basic Configuration   When you double-click on the GSNW Control Panel icon, you will see the Gateway Service for NetWare dialog box (see Figure 4.2).

The options that can be configured in the main dialog screen are defined in Table 4.2.

GSNW Gateway Configuration   To configure the GSNW gateway account, click on the Gateway button (see Figure 4.2). The GSNW Configure Gateway dialog box (see Figure 4.3) will appear.

In the Configure Gateway dialog box, you can configure the options shown in Table 4.3.

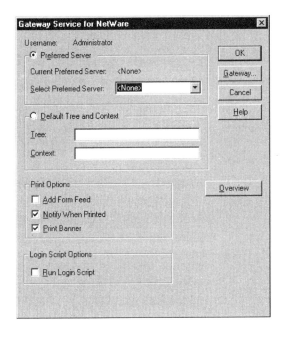

FIGURE 4.2

The Gateway Service for NetWare dialog box

TABLE 4.2

Gateway Service for NetWare Configuration Options Defined

GSNW Option	Description
Preferred Server	Used to specify the default NetWare server that you will connect to. This is used to specify a NetWare 2.x or 3.x server
Default Tree and Context	Used to specify a default tree and context. Tree and context are associated with Novell Directory Services (NDS) that is used by NetWare 4.x servers
Print Options	Defines the print options that will be used when NT gateway users send print jobs to NetWare print queues. You can specify if 'form feed', 'notify when done', or 'print banner' functions are enabled or disabled
Login Script Options	Specifies whether or not NetWare login scripts will be used by the gateway users when accessing the NetWare resources

FIGURE 4.3

The GSNW Configure
Gateway dialog box

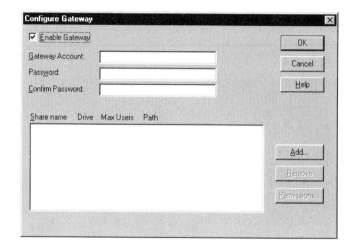

TABLE 4.3

GSNW Configure Gate-
way Configuration
Options

Configure Gateway Option	Explanation
Enable Gateway	Checked, this box enables the gateway. Unchecked, the gateway is disabled
Gateway Account	Used to specify the NetWare user account that has been configured as the gateway account and is a member of the NetWare group NTGATEWAY
Password and Confirm Password	Specify the NetWare Gateway account user password
Share box	Allows you to configure or modify shares of Net-Ware file resources for the gateway users

In this section, you learned how to provide connectivity to NetWare file and print resources. In the next section, you will learn how to migrate information from a NetWare server to an NT server.

Migration Tool for NetWare

The Migration Tool for NetWare is used to migrate specific objects from a NetWare server to an NT server. This is typically used when a NetWare server is being replaced by an NT server. The following sections will cover:

- Items that can and can't be migrated
- The prerequisites to using the Migration Tool for NetWare
- Running and configuring the Migration Tool for NetWare

Objects That Can Be Migrated

The Migration Tool for NetWare can be configured to migrate specific NetWare objects from NetWare to NT. You can migrate NetWare 2.x, 3.x, or 4.x servers.

It is important to note that the Migration Tool for NetWare does not support NetWare 4 NDS or Novell Directory Services. This means you must be running in bindery emulation to migrate from a NetWare 4.x NDS server.

The following NetWare items can or cannot be migrated.

NetWare Items That Can Be Migrated

- User accounts
- Group accounts
- Directories and files that you specify
- NetWare permissions on the directories and files that are migrated

In order for file and directory permissions to be migrated, the destination NT directory must be NTFS.

NetWare Items That Cannot Be Migrated

- User passwords
- Login scripts
- Print queues and print servers
- User Account Manager and Workgroup Manager specification

Prerequisites to Using the Migration Tool for NetWare

In order to use the Migration Tool for NetWare, the following requirements must first be met:

- You must be logged in with administrative rights on the NetWare side and on the NT side.

- You must be migrating to an NT domain controller if you are migrating user and group information.

- The NWLink IPX/SPX Compatible transport protocol must be installed on the NT server.

- The NT server must have GSNW installed.

Running and Configuring the Migration Tool for NetWare

Once you have met the prerequisites for running the Migration Tool for Net-Ware, you can run this utility from Start ➢ Programs ➢ Administrative Tools (Common) ➢ Migration Tool for NetWare.

The utility can also be run from the command line as boot drive:\WINNT\ SYSTEM32\NWCONV.EXE if desired.

The Migration Tool for NetWare dialog box (see Figure 4.4) will appear.

F I G U R E   4.4

The Migration Tool for NetWare dialog box

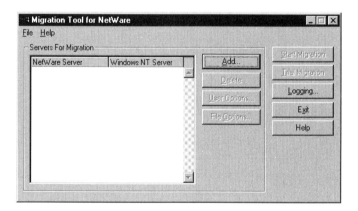

The first option you will configure is the source NetWare server and the destination NT server. Once you have selected the servers that will be used in the Migration, you can then configure the User and Group options, the File Options, Trial or Actual migration, and the Logging options that will be used for the migration.

User and Group Migration Options   Once you have selected the servers that will participate in the migration, the User Options button that was shown in Figure 4.4 will become active. If you click on this button, you will see the dialog box shown in Figure 4.5. From this screen, you can select to configure:

FIGURE 4.5

The User and Groups dialog box from Migration Tool for NetWare

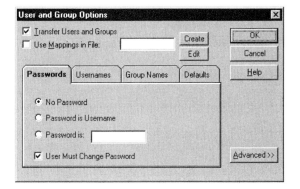

- That users and groups will or will not be transferred

- Whether or not a mapping file will be used

- How passwords should be specified for transferred users

- How usernames will be specified if duplication exists

- How group names will be specified if duplication exists

- How NetWare and NT account policies should be merged

Transfer Users and Groups

In Figure 4.5, the first check box, Transfer Users and Groups, is used to specify if NetWare users and groups will be transferred. If you select this box, then you can configure all of the following options.

Mapping File

The Use Mappings in File check box specifies whether or not a mapping file should be used. The mapping file is used to specify how users, groups, and passwords will be used on the NT server. If a mapping file has not been created, a new one will be opened and can be edited at this point.

For example, let's assume that you have a user Kevin Smith who has a user account named Kevin on the NetWare server. You can specify that Kevin will be transferred to the NT server as SmithK. Additionally, you can specify that his password will be 'buzz' through the use of a mapping file. This is the most user intensive method, but provides the best continuity of password security during the migration process.

Password Specification

As noted earlier, passwords can not be transferred from the NetWare side to the NT side. So, unless you specify the use of a mapping file that has password data, you must specify what will happen to the user's passwords. The choices are defined in Table 4.4.

TABLE 4.4 Password Options for the NetWare Migration	Password Option	Description
	No Password	Users will have no initial password on the NT server
	Password is Username	All users will have their migrated username as their initial password
	Password is:	Specifies a generic password that will be used initially by all of the users that were migrated from the NetWare server

None of these options are secure, so it's a good idea to use the mapping file.

Duplicate Usernames

It's possible to have an existing name on the NT domain that matches a name that exists on the NetWare server that is being migrated. Since NT does not allow duplicate user names, you can specify what will happen in this event through the Usernames tab in the Users and Groups dialog box. Table 4.5 lists your options.

T A B L E 4.5 Duplicate Username Resolution in a NetWare Migration	**Username Option**	**Description**
	Log Error	Specifies that an error should be reported in the ERROR.LOG file
	Ignore	Causes no action to be taken, so if you were migrating a user that already existed, the migration would ignore the new user in favor of the existing NT user
	Overwrite with new Info	Specifies that if a user already exists on the NT side, and a conflict exists, the NT user should be overwritten with the NetWare user
	Add Prefix	Specifies that the prefix you select should be added to the NetWare user account if a conflict exists. For example, Kevin might have the prefix NW added and become NWKevin. Since NT usernames can be changed, this is the preferred method of transfer

Duplicate Group Names

You specify how duplicate group names should be handled through the Group Names tab of the User and Group Options dialog box. The options that you can configure are:

- Log error
- Ignore
- Add prefix

These options are similar to the username options that were defined in Table 4.5.

Account Policy Defaults

The Defaults tab of the User and Group Options dialog box is used to specify how account management should be handled during the migration. The options you can choose from are shown in Table 4.6.

	Account Policy	Description
T A B L E 4.6 Account Defaults during NetWare Migration	Use Supervisor Defaults	Specifies that default NetWare account restrictions will be applied as opposed to the default NT account restrictions. This includes things like NT account policy criteria like minimum password and password expiration date
	Add Supervisors to the Administrators Group	This option is used to add NetWare Supervisor equivalents to the NT Administrators local group on the domain controller

File Options for Migration   Once you have selected the servers that will participate in the migration, the File Options button that was shown in Figure 4.4, becomes active. By clicking on this button, you will see the screen shown in Figure 4.6.

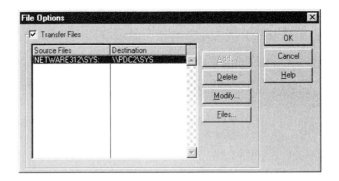

F I G U R E 4.6

The File Options dialog box for NetWare migration

Within the File Options dialog box, click the Transfer Files box to specify that you want to transfer directories and files. Once this box is checked, you can specify the directories and files you want to migrate as well as the destination directory.

When choosing the destination directory, you can specify that a new share be created and the properties of the destination directory. As noted earlier, if you want NetWare permissions to be migrated, you must select an NTFS partition as your destination directory.

Trial or Actual Migration   Before you perform the actual NetWare migration, you should perform a trial migration. A trial migration goes through all of the steps of a real migration, but does not actually transfer any data. This allows you to see if any errors will occur, and give you a chance to correct those errors before an actual migration is performed. Conduct as many trial migrations as required, until the trial runs error-free or produces errors that cannot be resolved.

Logging Options for Migration   During the NetWare migration, you can choose what logging information will be recorded. You can choose from:

- Pop-up Errors which will produce a pop-up box every time an error is encountered

- Verbose User/Group Logging which provides verbose information on users and groups transferred

- Verbose File Logging which provides verbose information on file and directory migrations

Now that you have learned about NetWare connectivity, we'll move on to Remote Access Server connectivity.

Remote Access Server

Remote access allows you to access remote network resources or access the main network from a remote location. NT does this through remote access server service and remote access client service. The remote access server software ships with NT Server and is called Remote Access Server, or RAS. The remote access client software ships with NT Workstation, Windows 95, and Windows for Workgroups and installs as a service that is accessed through Dial-up Networking on NT/95 operating systems. The NT Server CD also provides remote client software for other clients.

Installing RAS is fairly easy. It consists of two main steps:

1. Installing the RAS service from Control Panel ➤ Network ➤ Services

2. Installing and configuring the communication devices that RAS will use

In this section, you will learn about RAS communications, RAS protocols, RAS security, and RAS dial-up clients.

RAS Communications

RAS servers support a variety of communication options. You can communicate through:

- PSTN
- ISDN
- X.25
- RS-232 null modem cables
- PPTP

Each of these communication options are defined in Table 4.7.

TABLE 4.7 RAS Communication Options Defined	RAS Communication Type	Description
	PSTN	PSTN is the Public Switched Telephone Network and using PSTN is associated with good old analog modems
	ISDN	ISDN stands for Integrated Services Digital Network and is associated with digital communications. Instead of using modems with ISDN, you use ISDN adapters
	X.25	X.25 refers to a packet switching network that uses the X.25 protocol. X.25 networks have been declining in popularity as the Internet has taken over in popularity

	RAS Communication Type	Description
T A B L E 4.7 *(cont.)* RAS Communication Options Defined	RS-232 null modem cables	Serial cable used to connect two computers together. The cable is specially configured so that the transmit and receive wires are crossed on one side. This method could be used to test and troubleshoot RAS by removing the communication hardware from the connection path
	PPTP	PPTP is Point-to-Point Tunneling Protocol and is used to support RAS via Internet connections. PPTP can be a cost effective way of supporting long distance connections since you are able to take advantage of the Internet's infrastructure

RAS Protocols

RAS supports WAN protocols and LAN protocols. The WAN protocols that are supported are:

The WAN protocols supported through RAS are:

- SLIP (Serial Line Internet Protocol)
- PPP (Point-to-Point protocol)

The LAN protocols supported through RAS are:

- NetBEUI
- IPX
- TCP/IP

These protocols are described in the following subsections.

WAN Protocols

The WAN protocols associated with RAS are SLIP and PPP.

SLIP   SLIP is an older protocol that was originally developed for UNIX computers. It is not commonly used in Microsoft networks. RAS can use SLIP as a dial-out protocol, but it does not support SLIP for dialin connections. The disadvantages of SLIP are:

- No error checking
- No security
- No flow control or data compression

PPP   PPP is the default WAN protocol that is used when you install RAS. It offers the following benefits:

- Supports encrypted logons
- Supports NetBEUI, IPX, and TCP/IP
- Optimized for low-bandwidth connections

LAN Protocols

The LAN protocols supported through the RAS server are NetBEUI, IPX, and TCP/IP.

This section will cover the configuration option that is used by all three protocols, then look at specific configurations for each protocol.

To configure the LAN protocols you select Control Panel ➤ Network ➤ Services, then check the protocol you want to configure and click on the Configure button.

Common Configuration for All Protocols   Each network protocol can be configured to allow access to the Entire Network or This Computer Only.

The Entire Network option allows RAS clients to act as clients to the network. The client can access any network resources to which the user account has permissions.

The This Computer Only option only allows users to access resources on the RAS server only. This provides better security for the rest of the network.

NetBEUI   As noted in Unit 1, NetBEUI is simplest network protocol and requires the least amount of overhead. If your clients do not require the services of IPX or TCP/IP, NetBEUI will provide the best performance.

Other than the entire network or this computer only option, NetBEUI requires no configuration.

IPX As shown in Figure 4.7, the IPX protocol requires more configuration. The configuration options for IPX are defined in Table 4.8.

FIGURE 4.7

The RAS Server IPX Configuration dialog box

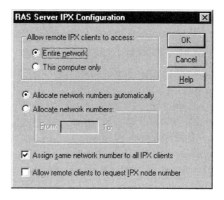

TABLE 4.8

RAS Server IPX Configuration Options Defined

RAS IPX Configuration Option	Description
Allocate network numbers automatically	Default option used to assign any IPX network number that is not in use by the RAS server
Allocate network numbers	Allows you to specify the range of network numbers. You provide the start range and the end range will be filled in automatically based on the number of ports you have defined
Assign same network numbers to all IPX clients	Specifies that only one network address be used by all RAS clients. This option helps reduce RIP traffic
Allow remote clients to request IPX node number	Allows remote clients to pick their own network address. You run a security risk with this option since a client can impersonate another node with the same address

TCP/IP TCP/IP is the most commonly used protocol. The TCP/IP configuration box is shown in Figure 4.8 and the configuration options are defined in Table 4.9.

F I G U R E   4.8

The RAS Server
TCP/IP Configuration
dialog box

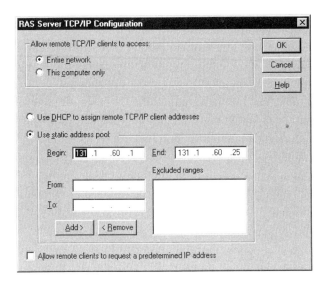

TABLE 4.9	RAS TCP/IP Configuration Option	Description
RAS Server TCP/IP Configuration Options Defined	Use DHCP to assign remote TCP/IP client addresses	Allows an RAS client to get an IP address from a DHCP server. If a DHCP server is not available, you must use the next option
	Use static address pool	Allows the assignment of IP addresses from a pool that you define. The pool requires an address for the network adapter in the RAS server and an IP address for each RAS client. The range must be valid for the subnet where the RAS server is located
	Allow remote clients to request a predetermined IP address	Allows the RAS clients to select their own IP address. This address must be valid for the subnet where the RAS server is located

TCP/IP is the only protocol that supports the Windows Sockets API. If your users require access to applications that use the Windows Sockets API, then you must configure TCP/IP for your RAS server and if you are using multiple protocols, it should be listed first in the bindings order.

RAS Security

You can make your RAS server more secure by applying security dictating, for instance, who can use RAS, dial-back requirements and encryption methods.

Specifying Authorized RAS Users and RAS Call Back

One of the first steps in setting up RAS security is determining who should be able to use RAS and if any call back options should be applied.

You can specify if a user is authorized for RAS through:

- Remote Access Admin (shown in Figure 4.9)

- User Manager for Domains (through the Dialin property box of each user)

The Remote Access Admin utility can be used to manage the RAS communication ports; start, stop, and pause the RAS service; or assign RAS permissions. To assign RAS permissions, you select Users ➤ Permissions.

FIGURE 4.9

The Remote Access
Permissions dialog box

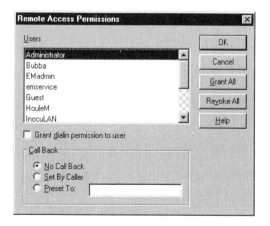

The same dialog box that is used to specify dialin permissions is used to specify call back security. Call back security is defined in Table 4.10.

T A B L E 4.10	**Call Back Option**	**Description**
RAS Call Back Security Defined	No Call Back	Call back is not used
	Set By Caller	The caller specifies the number that will be called back. This option is often used so that the caller does not bear costs of long distance calls and that remote access locations can be tracked
	Preset To	This option specifies the number that will be called back. This option is used for accounts that are sensitive, such as administrative accounts, that will always RAS in from a fixed location

RAS Encryption

As noted earlier, RAS encryption is supported for PPP clients. You can configure RAS encryption through Control Panel ➢ Network ➢ Services ➢ Remote Access Service ➢ Properties. Once you access the dialog box shown in Figure 4.10, you can choose from:

- Allow any authentication including clear text
- Require encrypted authentication
- Require Microsoft encrypted authentication

These options are described in Table 4.11.

RAS Dial-Up Clients

Once the RAS server has been installed, you must install the RAS client software. Depending on the client platform you are using, setup will differ. This section will focus on how to install and configure an NT RAS client.

FIGURE 4.10

The Remote Access Service Network Configuration dialog box

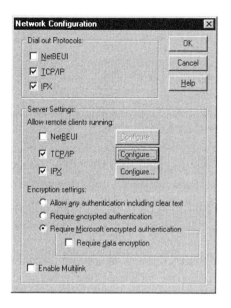

TABLE 4.11

RAS Encryption Options Defined

RAS Encryption	Description
Allow any authentication including clear text	The least secure method, but supports many levels of encryption including MS-CHAP, SPAP, and PAP. This option is useful if you have a variety of clients dialing in and you want to support whatever encryption they are using
Require encrypted authentication	Supports the MS-CHAP and SPAP encryption methods, but not PAP. This method requires that clients use encrypted passwords
Require Microsoft encrypted authentication	The most secure encryption method. This option uses MS-CHAP encryption and is the only encryption option that also allows you to specify that data should be encrypted in addition to the user's password

Installing RAS Client Software

To install the RAS client software on an NT client, you choose the My Computer icon from the desktop, then click the Dial-up Networking icon. You will specify:

- A phone book entry (where you'll call your RAS server)

- The communication device you'll use

- The telephony dialing properties (where you are calling from)

During the installation of the RAS client software (also called dial-up networking or DUN), you can also configure your RAS connection, which is covered in the next section.

Configuring RAS Client Software

Once the Dial-up networking software has been installed, you will see the screen shown in Figure 4.11. To configure the client software click the More button shown in Figure 4.11, and choose the Edit Entries and modem properties selection. You will see the figure shown in Figure 4.12.

FIGURE 4.11

The Dial-Up Networking dialog box

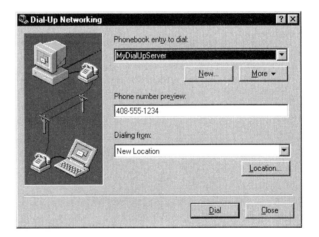

FIGURE 4.12

The Edit Phonebook
Entry dialog box

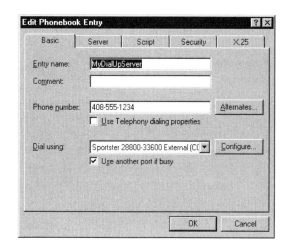

From the dialog box shown in Figure 4.12, you can configure the client DUN properties. Two of the most important configuration tabs are:

- Server

- Security

These tabs are covered in the following subsections.

Server Tab   As shown in Figure 4.13, the Server tab allows you to configure the connection for the server that you will connect to. These options are defined in Table 4.12.

FIGURE 4.13

The Dial-up Network-
ing Server property tab

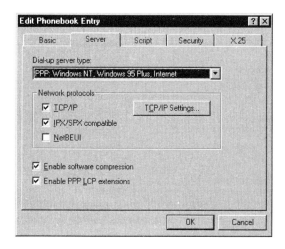

T A B L E 4.12	**Server Option**	**Description**
Dial-up Networking Server Property Tab Options Defined	Dial-up server type	Allows you to specify if you are using a PPP connection to attach to Windows NT, Windows 95 Plus, or the Internet, a SLIP connection to the Internet, or a connection to a Windows NT 3.1 or Windows for Workgroups computer
	Network Protocols	Allows you to specify the dialin protocol(s) you will use. You can choose from TCP/IP, IPX/SPX compatible, or Net-BEUI. You must have a protocol in common with the RAS server you are calling
	Enable software compression	Offers software compression that is used in addition to modem hardware compression
	Enable PPP LCP extensions	Specifies that you want to enable enhancement features for PPP. This can cause problems if you connect to a server running outdated PPP software

Security Tab   The security tab specifies the authentication and encryption you want to use. The options are shown in Figure 4.14 and defined in Table 4.13.

F I G U R E 4.14

The Dial-up Networking Security Property Tab

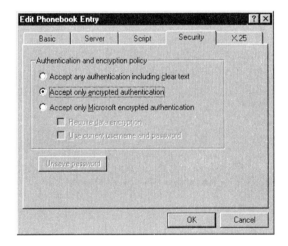

T A B L E 4.13	**Authentication Option**	**Description**
Dial-up Networking Security Property Tab Options Defined	Accept any authentication including clear text	Specifies that the client can specify any authentication that is requested by the server, including no authentication (which could happen if you were connecting to a non-Microsoft server)
	Accept only encrypted authentication	Specifies that you can authenticate with any encryption method except PAP. This is more secure than the previous option
	Accept only Microsoft encrypted authentication	Specifies that you want to use the MS-CHAP encryption method to authenticate. This assumes that you will connect to a Microsoft server. This is the most secure authentication method and allows you the option of also encrypting any data that is sent

Now that you've reviewed NT connectivity, it's time to put your knowledge to the test.

NetWare Connectivity

1. The _____ service is used to allow users who are attached to an NT server to access NetWare file and print resources.

2. What group must be created on the NetWare server to allow the NetWare gateway to be functional?

_____

3. What pre-requisite must be met on the NT server before GSNW can be installed?

_____

4. If you have six NT users and five Windows 95 users who are accessing a NetWare server through an NT server running GSNW, how many user connections will they use on the NetWare server?

_____

5. True or False. The Migration Tool for NetWare can be used to migrate NT users and groups to a NetWare server.

6. True or False. User passwords can be migrated with the Migration Tool for NetWare.

7. True or False. User accounts can be migrated with the Migration Tool for NetWare.

8. True or False. Directories and files can be migrated with the Migration Tool for NetWare.

9. True or False. Login scripts can be migrated with the Migration Tool for NetWare.

10. True or False. Print queues can be migrated with the Migration Tool for NetWare.

11. True or False. NetWare permissions on directories and files can be migrated with the Migration Tool for NetWare.

12. What is the requirement that must be met if you want your files and permissions transferred with your directories and files during a NetWare migration?

_____

13. What is the most secure way to specify user passwords for users who are migrated through a NetWare migration?

_____

14. True or False. NetWare users and groups can be migrated to an NT domain controller or member server using the Migration Tool for NetWare.

15. The _____ protocol and the _____ _____ service must be running on the NT server before you use Migration Tool for NetWare.

16. True or False. GSNW can be used to allow NetWare users to access NT file and print resources.

17. The _____ protocol can be used to provide access to NetWare servers running NetBIOS applications.

18. In order for NetWare clients to access NT file and print resources, you must install the _____ _____ protocol and the _____ _____ service on your NT server.

19. How do you test a NetWare migration without making any changes on either of your servers?

_____

20. Assume that you have a user named Terry on your NT server and your NetWare server that will be used in a NetWare migration. Which username option would you choose if you wanted Terry's account on the NT server to be overwritten with the account from the NetWare server?

_____

21. Assume that you have a user named Ron on your NT server and your NetWare server that will be used in a NetWare migration. Which username option would you choose if you wanted Ron's account on the NT server to be used and the NetWare account to be discarded during the migration process?

_____

22. What service should you install on an NT server if a user will log on locally at the server and requires access to NetWare file and print resources?

_____

23. True or False. You can configure the NetWare Preferred Server in the main GSNW properties dialog box.

24. True or False. You can configure the NetWare default tree and context in the main GSNW properties dialog box.

25. True or False. You can configure the NetWare print options in the main GSNW properties dialog box.

26. True or False. You can configure the NetWare file access in the main GSNW properties dialog box.

27. True or False. You can configure the NetWare mapped network drives in the main GSNW properties dialog box.

28. True or False. You can configure the NetWare login script options in the main GSNW properties dialog box.

29. In order to run the Migration Tool for NetWare, which group or groups should your user account on the NT server have membership in?

_____

30. How do you install GSNW?

_____

31. When you configure the NT gateway, what information should go into the Gateway account information box, and where does this account exist?

_____

32. By checking the _____ account policy, you allow NetWare supervisor equivalents to become members of the NT Domain Administrators group during a NetWare migration.

33. If you want the NetWare account policies to override the NT account policies, you check the _____ account policy option when you configure the NetWare migration.

34. List the three logging options you can select during a NetWare migration.

_____

_____

_____

Remote Access Server

35. List the five communication methods that are supported by RAS.

_____

_____

_____

_____

_____

36. List the two utilities that can be used to grant a user permission to dial in to your RAS server.

_____

_____

37. The _____ callback option provides the highest level of security.

38. The _____ RAS encryption option offers the highest level of security.

39. _____ is the default WAN protocol used by RAS because it supports dial out and dialin connections as well as encryption.

40. The _____ WAN protocol is not widely used and NT RAS does not support it being used for dialin connections.

41. The _____ LAN protocol used with RAS provides the least amount of overhead.

42. If you had traveling users, who connected via RAS from various locations, yet still wanted to use callback, which option would you use?

_____

43. The _____ protocol must be installed on your RAS server if you will be supporting remote access to applications that use the Windows Sockets API.

44. If you are configuring TCP/IP for RAS and you specify that you will use a static address pool, other than IP addresses, what IP configuration can be configured on the RAS server?

_____

45. True or False. The following authentication methods can be used with the RAS Require encrypted authentication option.

_____ MS-CHAP

_____ SPAP

_____ PAP

46. True or False. A RAS client can call into an NT server running RAS with the SLIP protocol.

47. The Require Microsoft encrypted authentication option specifies that the _____ _____ encryption method be used.

48. If you want all data to be encrypted, including passwords and data, which encryption method(s) can be used?

_____

49. True or False. If a Microsoft NT RAS client specified that they were using Accept any authentication including clear text and the NT RAS server specified Require Microsoft encrypted authentication, the client could connect to the RAS server.

50. List the three LAN protocols that can be used by RAS.

_____

_____

_____

4-1 Your network has a variety of clients including NT Workstations, Windows 95 computers, and Windows for Workgroups clients. Each of the clients access network resources through Microsoft Networking redirector software. What can you install on your NT server to allow these users to access NetWare file and print resources?

   A. Install the CSNW software.

   B. Install the File and Print Services for NetWare software.

   C. Install the GSNW software.

   D. You only need the NWLink protocol installed on the NT server.

4-2 Your company is a large accounting firm. Some of the accountants work on-site with clients, but still need to access corporate resources. You have proposed to setup a RAS server so that the accountants can dial in to your network from their Windows 95 notebook computers. You are very concerned that all of the remote transmissions be secure. In order to have the project approved, you require that all passwords and data be encrypted during transmission. How should you configure the RAS server security?

   A. Require encrypted authentication.

   B. Require Microsoft encrypted authentication.

   C. Require secure sockets layer (SSL) encryption.

   D. Require C-2/E-2 compliant encryption services.

4-3 You have configured your NT server with the TCP/IP, NetBEUI, and NWLink protocols. No services other than the default service have been installed. Based on this configuration, which of the following access scenarios are possible?

    A. NetWare users can access NT File and Print resources.

    B. An NT user who is sitting at the NT server can access NetWare file and print resources.

    C. Any users who are attached to the NT server can access NetWare file and print resources.

    D. NT users can access NetWare server NetBIOS applications.

4-4 Your network consists of a large mixture of NT servers and NetWare servers. The MIS department has been using NetWare servers, but has decided to switch to NT servers. However, you don't want to start from scratch. You have decided to use the Migration Tool for NetWare. What software must be loaded on the NT server that will participate in the NetWare migration?

    A. CSNW

    B. GSNW

    C. File and Print Services for NetWare

    D. NWGS

4-5 Your company uses a RAS server so that users can dial in and access network resources remotely. Some of the users dial in from fixed locations and other users travel to multiple locations. You want the highest level of security possible. What is the best call back security to implement?

    A. Call back is implemented on a per-user basis. For the users who dial in from multiple locations, select the Set by Caller option. For the users who dial in from fixed locations, select the Preset to option.

B. Call back is implemented on a per-port basis. Setup two ports for users that dial in. Configure one port for the call back option set by caller. Configure another port with the Preset to call back option. Direct users to call into the appropriate port.

C. Call back is implemented as a global policy on the RAS server. Because some users call in from multiple locations, you should define the Set by caller call back option.

D. Set call back for the NT server to allow any call back option and instruct users to specify secure call back during the client connection.

4-6   Your company uses NT. Recently a corporate policy was implemented that allows certain users to telecommute every other Friday. You have decided to implement a RAS server so that these users can access network resources. You have two issues. You want the highest level of security, but users will be using their own personal computers and you have no way of knowing what platform or software they are using to dial in with. While security is important, access is even more important. Based on this information, what encryption option should you select?

A. Allow any authentication including clear text.

B. Require encrypted authentication.

C. Require C2/E2 compliant encryption.

D. Require Microsoft encrypted authentication.

4-7   You have just installed and configured a RAS server. During the test phase, you tried to dial in and log on as a user named Kaitlin, but the connection was unsuccessful. The error message indicated that Kaitlin does not have RAS permissions. Which utility or utilities can be used to grant RAS dial-in permissions?

A. Control Panel ➤ Network ➤ Services ➤ Remote Access Server ➤ Properties

B. User Manager for Domains

C. Remote Access Admin

D. Server Manager

SAMPLE TEST

4-8   You are in the process of installing and configuring RAS on your NT server. During the configuration process, you chose to use the TCP/IP protocol. When configuring TCP/IP, you selected the Use static address pool option. Which of the following options can you configure with this configuration?

    A. IP addresses

    B. Default gateway

    C. Subnet mask

    D. WINS server

    E. DNS server

4-9   Your network consists of a mixture of NT and NetWare servers. You want to provide your NT users with access to NetWare file and print resources. You decide to install GSNW on one of your NT servers. In order to configure the gateway, which of the following steps are required?

    A. You must load the GSNW NLM on the NetWare server.

    B. You must create a group called NTGATEWAY on the NT server.

    C. You must create a group called NTGATEWAY on the NetWare server.

    D. You must create a group called NWGATEWAY on the NT server.

    E. You must create a group called NWGATEWAY on the NetWare server.

4-10   Your network consists of a mixture of NT and NetWare servers. You want to provide your NT users with access to NetWare file and print resources. You decide to install GSNW on one of your NT servers. During the configuration of GSNW, you configure the gateway. What should be specified in the Gateway Account box?

    A. An administrator account on the NetWare server

    B. An administrator account in the NT server

C. A user account that belongs to the NTGATEWAY group on the NetWare server

D. A user account that belongs to the NWGATEWAY account on the NT server

4-11 Your company consists of 100 employees. Half of the company is based in Houston where you have a corporate office. The other 50 employees are remote sales people who are spread around the country. The users currently dial in to your RAS server using long distance connections with analog modems. What protocol would allow the users to access your RAS server through an Internet connection so that your company can save on their long distance charges?

A. PPP

B. ISDN

C. X.25

D. PPTP

4-12 You are configuring a Windows 95 computer that will be used to dial in to an NT server using RAS. Which of the following WAN protocols can be used to dial in? Choose all that apply.

A. PPP

B. SLIP

C. TCP/IP

D. IPX/SPX

4-13 Your network consists of a mixture of NT and NetWare servers. Your NetWare users would like to be able to access some of the NT file and print resources. What software should be installed to allow this access?

A. GSNW on the NT server

B. File and Print Services for NetWare on the NT server

C. File and Print Service for NetWare on the NetWare server

D. The GSNW NLM on the NetWare server

4-14   You are configuring a Windows 95 computer that will be used to dial in to a UNIX server. You want to use the protocol with the lowest amount of overhead. What WAN protocol should you use?

    A. PPP

    B. SLIP

    C. TCP/IP

    D. IPX/SPX

4-15   The accounting department standardized on NetWare servers five years ago. The decision has been made to now use an NT network. You are in charge of migrating the NetWare servers to NT servers. How should you configure Migration Tool for NetWare so that the most secure passwords will be applied?

    A. Transfer the NetWare passwords during the migration.

    B. Specify that random passwords will be generated.

    C. Specify the password is: option and specify a secure password for each user.

    D. Use the mapping file option.

4-16   You are supporting an NT server that will be used for remote access. You install a RAS server. What LAN protocols can be installed?

    A. NetBEUI

    B. NWLink

    C. IPX/SPX

    D. TCP/IP

    E. AFP

SAMPLE TEST

4-17 You are supporting an NT server that will be used for remote access. During the planning stage you are in the process of deciding what type of connections you will support. Which of the following RAS communication methods can you choose from?

A. PSTN

B. ISDN

C. V.24

D. X.500

E. X.25

F. PPTP

G. PSDN

4-18 Your network consists of a mixture of NT and NetWare servers. You decide to migrate one of the NetWare servers to an NT server through the Migration Tool for NetWare utility. What is the best option for minimizing the errors that will occur during migration?

A. First, perform a trial migration(s).

B. Choose the Pop-up errors logging option.

C. Choose the Verbose User/Group logging option.

D. Choose the Verbose File logging option.

4-19 You have decided to migrate a NetWare server to an NT server using the Migration Tool for NetWare. You will be migrating NetWare user and group accounts. Which of the following requirements apply to the NT server?

A. The server must have an NTFS partition.

B. The server can be an NT member server.

C. The server can be an NT domain controller.

D. You must be logged in as a user who is a member of the Server Operators group or the Administrators group.

4-20 You have decided to migrate a NetWare server to an NT server using the Migration Tool for NetWare. You will be migrating NetWare directories and permissions. Which of the following requirements apply to the NT server?

    A. The server must have an NTFS partition.

    B. The server can be an NT member server.

    C. The server can be an NT domain controller.

    D. You must be logged in as a user who is a member of the Server Operators group or the Administrators group.

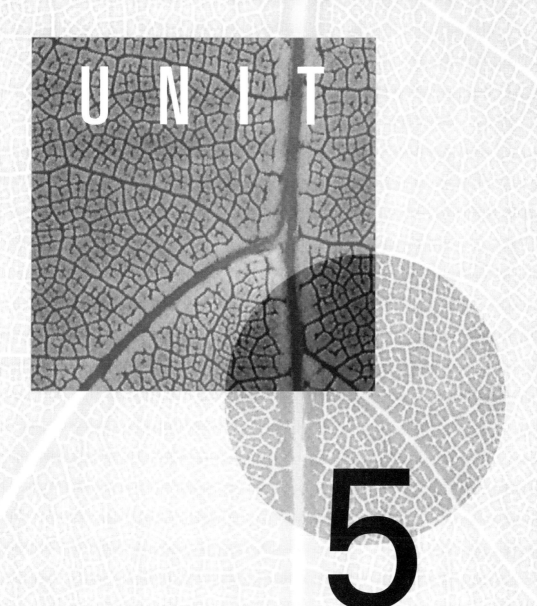

UNIT

5

Monitoring and Optimization

Test Objectives: Monitoring and Optimization

■ Monitor performance of various functions by using Performance Monitor. Functions include:

- Processor
- Memory
- Disk
- Network

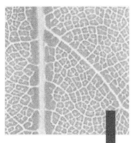

In the following sections, you will learn how Performance Monitor works to optimize NT Server performance.

Monitoring and Optimization

The Performance Monitor utility is used to manage and optimize NT servers.

This unit will overview how Performance Monitor is organized, key components to track, and the views that can be selected through Performance Monitor.

Organization of Performance Monitor

Performance Monitor is organized in a hierarchical structure. You track performance by selecting items you want to monitor. The top level of the structure is Computer (see Figure 5.1), which is broken down into Objects, which are further broken down into Counters. These terms are defined in Table 5.1.

FIGURE 5.1

Organization of Performance Monitor

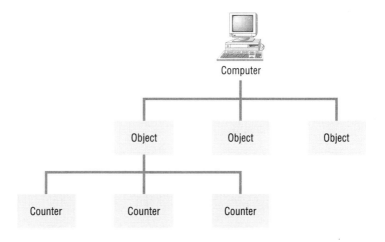

TABLE 5.1 Organization of Performance Monitor Defined	Organization Option	Description	Example
	Computer	Specifies the computer that you will monitor. You can monitor the local computer through Performance Monitor, or you can monitor remote computers, assuming that you have administrative rights to do so	Any computer's NetBIOS name
	Object	Each computer contains objects, the sum of which is the computer. There are default objects which exist in all NT computers, then there are objects that are present or not present depending on the computer's configuration	Cache, Logical Disk, Memory, Processor
	Counter	Counters further isolate specific areas within each object. For example, Memory is a fairly broad option. By further subdividing memory into discrete counters, you can track specific counters that relate to the area of memory you want to monitor	The object Memory contains counters for Available bytes, Pages per second, and the number of committed bytes

In addition, each object can also have multiple instances. For example, if you have two physical hard drives, you would have two instances of the object PhysicalDisk which would allow you to track each disk.

Key Server Components to Monitor

The key objects that you track through Performance Monitor are processor, memory, disk, and network.

Processor

The processor object is used to track how hard your CPU(s) are working. The key counters that you should watch are defined in Table 5.2.

TABLE 5.2 Processor Counters to Watch	Counter	Description	Undesirable Values	Likely Cause of Problem
	%Processor Time	The percentage of the time the processor is busy performing useful tasks	Above 80%	Not enough horsepower for the applications you are running. Either add another processor, upgrade the processor you have, or move applications to another server
	Interrupts per second	This is the number of device interrupts the processor is handling each second	Over 3,500 on a Pentium or RISC computer	Poorly written program or device driver, or a failing piece of hardware

Memory

Memory or lack thereof is one of the most likely bottlenecks you can encounter. Memory is broken up into two areas: your physical RAM and your page file.

The two counters that you should monitor to view your memory statistics are:

- The Cache object, Data Map Hits% counter

- The Memory object, Pages/Sec

The Data Map Hits% counter specifies the percentage of requests that can be processed through physical RAM as opposed to having to access the data from disk.

The Pages/Sec counter specifies the number of pages that were written or read from disk because the pages were not available through physical RAM, or cache memory.

If you suspect that lack of memory is the problem, add more physical RAM.

Disk

The first thing you should do to monitor disk performance is to enable disk counters by executing the DISKPERF -y command. Once this command has been issued, restart the computer for the disk counters to collect information.

Disk counters are tracked through the Physical Disk and Logical Disk objects. Physical Disk relates to the physical hard drive. For example, you might have two physical hard drives, drive 0 and drive 1. Logical Disk refers to the disk partition. For example, Disk 0 might be broken down into Logical Drive C: and Logical Drive D:. This is also referred to as disk partitions.

Table 5.3 defines the counters that you should add to monitor your disk's performance.

T A B L E 5.3 Performance Monitor Disk Counters	Object	Counter	Description
	LogicalDisk	Average Disk Queue Length	This is the average number of outstanding requests that the disk is waiting to process. This number should not exceed two
	LogicalDisk	% Disk Time	This is the percentage of time that the disk is busy processing read or write requests

If you suspect that the disk channel is the bottleneck, you can take the following actions:

- Use RAID 0 or RAID 5 to take advantage of disk striping.

- Use faster disks and disk controllers.

- Balance heavily used files by moving them to a less frequently used disk channel.

Network

You can monitor your network statistics through the NetBEUI, TCP/IP, and NWLink objects. The objects you track will be dependent on the protocols you are using.

It is important to note that in order to track the TCP/IP-related counters, you must first install the SNMP (Simple Network Management Protocol) service on the computer that you want to track TCP/IP statistics on. To install SNMP, add the service from Control Panel ➤ Network ➤ Services tab.

If you suspect that your network channel is the bottleneck, you should take the following action:

- Buy network adapter cards that take advantage of the full bus width on your computer.

- Segment busy networks into two or more subnets.

Performance Monitor Views

Performance Monitor offers four views that are used to track and analyze the data that you collect. The views are chart, alert, log, and report. These views are described in Table 5.4.

T A B L E 5.4 Performance Monitor Views Defined	View	Description
	Chart	Chart is the default view and displays what is being tracked in real-time. You can view the chart through a graph or a histogram
	Alert	Alert is used to specify threshold conditions that will trigger an alert. You specify an alert by choosing a counter, then specifying an alert generated by a threshold being over or under a value you define. In addition, you can specify an action that will be taken if an alert is generated
	Log	Log is used to save data to a log file. This is normally the view that would be used if you were creating a baseline for analysis or historical record
	Report	Report view textually reports the objects and counters that you have defined in real-time. This view is useful when you are tracking a large number of counters that are difficult to read through the chart view

Monitoring and Optimization

1. Which service must be used if you will be collecting statistics regarding TCP/IP?

_____

2. Which Performance Monitor view would you use if you were creating a baseline and wanted to compare the information you collected on a monthly basis?

_____

3. What is the most likely cause of poor performance on an NT server?

_____

4. In order to enable disk counters, what two steps should you take?

_____

_____

5. You might have a bottleneck if the %Processor Time counter were _____ _____ or higher.

6. What are the four most important objects that you should be concerned with when monitoring system performance?

_____

_____

_____

_____

7. The _____ view in Performance Monitor is used to track real-time information in a graph format.

8. List two possible hardware fixes to the processor as a bottleneck.

_____

_____

9. List two objects that can be used to view your memory statistics through Performance Monitor.

_____

_____

10. You want to be notified if the LogicalDisk, Average Disk Queue Length becomes greater than 2, what should you do?

_____

11. List three steps that can be taken to alleviate disk I/O problems.

_____

_____

_____

12. List the four Performance Monitor views.

_____

_____

_____

_____

5-1 You are the system administrator for a large NT network. Recently you have been concerned that your servers may not be performing at an optimal level. You decide to run Performance Monitor on your servers to see what is going on. One of the counters you track is %Processor Time. The average for this counter is 15%. Based on this value, what action(s) should you take?

A. Add a faster processor to the computer.

B. If the computer will support multiple processors, add another processor.

C. Add more memory to the computer.

D. Do nothing, the counter does not indicate a problem.

5-2 Your company is growing at a rapid rate. Currently you are adding 20 new users to your server every month. You have decided to use Performance Monitor to track the effect of the new users by creating baselines of usage every two weeks. Based on your baselines, you feel that you will be able to be pro-active in your maintenance of the server. When you configure Performance Monitor, which view should you select?

A. Graph

B. Report

C. Log

D. Baseline

E. Histograph

5-3 You are the administrator of an NT domain called SALES. Within the SALES domain, you have a PDC called SALESPDC. You have decided that you want to use Performance Monitor to track the PDCs performance. One of the main items you want to track is network performance. However, it is inconvenient for you to monitor the server locally. You decide to use Performance Monitor on your NT workstation, which is called NTWSADMIN. Your network uses the TCP/IP protocol. What do you need to configure for this scenario? Choose all that apply.

   A. Add the SNMP service on SALESPDC.

   B. Add the SNMP service on NTWSADMIN.

   C. Enable the Network Performance Monitor counter in SALESPDC.

   D. Configure the Network Performance Monitor counter on NTWSADMIN.

5-4 You are concerned that you have a lack of memory on your server that is causing slow performance. What Performance Monitor counter should you track?

   A. Memory object, Pages/Sec

   B. Paging File object, %Usage

   C. Cache object, %Usage

   D. Cache object, Pages/Sec

5-5 You are the administrator of an NT domain called SALES. Within the SALES domain, you have a PDC called SALESPDC. You have decided that you want to use Performance Monitor to track the PDCs performance. One of the main items you want to track is disk performance. However, it is inconvenient for you to monitor the server locally. You decide to use Performance Monitor on your NT workstation, which is called NTWSADMIN. What do you need to configure for this scenario? Choose all that apply.

   A. Run DISKPERF -y on SALESPDC and reboot.

   B. Run PERFMON -y on SALESPDC and reboot.

C. Run DISKPERF -y on NTWSADMIN and reboot.

D. Run PERFMON -y on NTWSADMIN and reboot.

5-6 You have configured Performance Monitor to track the Processor object, Interrupts per Second counter. You are concerned that the processor might be a bottleneck, and want to be proactive in your management if any problems are indicated. What is the best way to be notified if there is a problem?

A. Configure the Notification option in the Tools area of Performance Monitor.

B. Configure the Notification option in the Tools area of Server Manager.

C. Use the Notification view in Performance Monitor.

D. Use the Alert view in Performance Monitor.

5-7 You are the network administrator for a large accounting firm. The accounting firm uses a server called ACCTAPPS as an applications server. You have been receiving complaints from your users that the servers performance seems slow. You run Performance Monitor, and notice that the Memory object, Pages/Sec is double what it was last month. As this number grows, your performance keeps dropping. What is the best solution for this problem?

A. Create a larger paging file.

B. Split the paging file over multiple physical disks.

C. Split the paging file over multiple logical disks.

D. Add more RAM.

5-8 You have been monitoring your NT server through Performance Monitor. You have been monitoring the server over six months. The server is a Pentium with 64 MB of RAM. You have noticed that the Processor, Interrupts per Second counter has grown to 4,000. What are possible causes of this problem? Choose all that apply.

    A. There is not enough RAM.

    B. You need a faster processor.

    C. You have a failing piece of hardware.

    D. You have a poorly written device driver.

5-9 You have been tracking your servers performance for a period of six months. In that time, your computing needs have doubled. You have especially noticed that one bottleneck is in the network. Which of the following solutions might provide some relief? Choose all that apply.

    A. Segment the network.

    B. Buy network cards having larger bus widths.

    C. Add more RAM to your servers.

    D. Add faster processors to you servers.

5-10 You have just added a new application to your NT Server. You want to monitor the performance of the server using Performance Monitor. Which Performance Monitor view will allow you to monitor the performance through a real-time graph?

    A. Report

    B. Log

    C. Histograph

    D. Chart

UNIT

6

Troubleshooting

Test Objectives: Troubleshooting

- Choose the appropriate action to take to resolve installation failures.

- Choose the appropriate course of action to take to resolve boot failures.

- Choose the appropriate action to take to resolve configuration errors.

- Choose the appropriate course of action to take to resolve printer problems.

- Choose the appropriate course of action to take to resolve RAS problems.

- Choose the appropriate course of action to take to resolve connectivity problems.

- Choose the appropriate course of action to take to resolve resource access problems and permissions problems.

■ Choose the appropriate course of action to take to resolve fault-tolerance failures. Fault-tolerance methods include:

- Tape backup
- Mirroring
- Stripe set with parity
- Disk duplexing

Exam objectives are subject to change at any time without prior notice and at Microsoft's sole discretion. Please visit Microsoft's Training & Certification website (www.microsoft.com/Train_Cert) for the most current exam objectives listing.

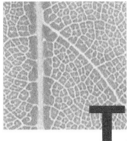

The following section will overview NT troubleshooting.

Troubleshooting Installation Errors

Installation errors can have many causes. Some of the common causes are:

- Media errors
- Hardware that is not on the HCL (hardware compatibility list)
- Incorrect hardware configuration
- Problems connecting to the domain controller
- Blue screen or stop messages

Table 6.1 contains tips for troubleshooting common installation errors.

TABLE 6.1 Common Installation Errors	Errors	Possible Solutions
	Media errors	You could have a bad floppy or the NT Server CD may be corrupt. If you suspect that you have media errors, create a different set of setup diskettes or try another NT Server CD
	Hardware not on the HCL	NT is picky about the hardware it uses. Verify that all of the hardware you are using is on the HCL
	Incorrect hardware configuration	Check hardware components such as network card, video adapter, sound card, modems, etc. for configuration settings. There must be no overlap in IRQs, base memory, base i/o addresses, or DMA. In addition, the software configurations must match the hardware configurations

TABLE 6.1 *(cont.)* Common Installation Errors	Errors	Possible Solutions
	Problems connecting to the domain controller	If you are installing a BDC or are joining a domain during installation, your computer will contact the PDC. Common errors that would prevent you from contacting the PDC are spelling the PDCs name incorrectly, incorrect network settings, or the PDC is not currently online
	Blue screen or stop messages	Blue screen or stop messages during installation can be caused by incorrect or outdated drivers being initialized. If this is a problem, don't let NT auto-detect your mass storage device. Instead manually identify the mass storage you are using, and provide the correct driver. You should be able to get the correct driver from the manufacturer's Web site

In the next section, you will learn how to identify and correct boot failures.

Troubleshooting Boot Failures

In troubleshooting boot failures, you must first identify which file is causing the boot error, then correct the problem.

NT Boot Files

The primary files that are used to boot NT on an Intel platform are:

- NTLDR
- BOOT.INI
- BOOTSECT.DOS
- NTDETECT.COM
- NTOSKRNL.EXE
- NTBOOTDD.SYS (SCSI Drives only)

These files are described in Table 6.2. Table 6.3 includes the error that will occur if there is a problem with the boot file.

TABLE 6.2 NT Boot Files	Boot File	Description
	NTLDR	This file is used to control the NT boot process after Power On Self Testing hardware routines are complete
	BOOT.INI	This configuration file is responsible for building the operating system menu choices that are displayed upon boot up. It provides the location on the boot partition that NT is installed on
	BOOTSECT.DOS	This file is used to load any operating system that was installed prior to NT. This file is loaded if you choose an alternate operating system during the boot process
	NTDETECT.COM	This file is used to detect installed hardware and add the hardware it detects to the registry if an NT operating system was selected
	NTOSKRNL.EXE	This is the NT kernel

If you are using an SCSI controller with the BIOS disabled, you also need the NTBOOTDD.SYS file.

TABLE 6.3 Boot File Failure Messages	Boot File	Error Message if File is Missing or Corrupt
	NTLDR	Boot: Couldn't find NTLDR. Please insert another disk.
	BOOT.INI	Windows NT could not start because the following file is missing or corrupt: winnt\system32\ntoskrnl.exe. Please re-install a copy of the above file.

T A B L E 6.3 *(cont.)*	**Boot File**	**Error Message if File is Missing or Corrupt**
Boot File Failure Messages	BOOTSECT.DOS	I\O Error accessing boot sector file multi(0)disk(0)rdisk(0)partition(1):\bootsect.dos
	NTDETECT.COM	NTDETECT v1.0 Checking Hardware... NTDETECT v1.0 Checking Hardware...
	NTOSKRNL.EXE	Windows NT could not start because the following file is missing or corrupt: winnt\system32\ ntoskrnl.exe. Please re-install a copy of the above file.

If you have used Disk Administrator and your system fails to boot, suspect the BOOT.INI file first. By adding logical partitions, you can cause the ARC name to change. When using Disk Administrator, pay careful attention to the exit messages, because you will be warned if the BOOT.INI needs to be edited, and if so, what the edits should be. Users often ignore this message.

Recovery of NT Boot Files

If any of your boot files are missing or corrupt, you can repair the failure through the emergency repair disk (ERD). To repair your boot files, you will need the three NT setup disks and the ERD.

- If you do not already have the setup disks you can create them from the Windows NT Server CD by typing WINNT /ox.

- To create the ERD, you type RDISK from a command prompt on the computer the ERD is being created for.

The steps to recover your boot files are as follows:

1. When prompted, boot with the NT Setup Boot disks. Insert Disk 1 and Disk 2.

2. When prompted, choose R for Repair.

3. When prompted, insert Setup Disk 3.

4. As requested, insert the ERD.

5. Select the Verify Windows NT System Files option.

6. Select the components you wish to restore.

Now your NT boot files should be properly restored.
In the next section, you will learn how to troubleshoot configuration errors.

Troubleshooting Configuration Errors

Configuration errors come in many sizes and shapes. NT has a variety of utilities that can be used to identify and correct configuration errors. These utilities include:

- The Event Viewer

- Server Manager

- Windows NT Diagnostics

- The Last Known Good Option

- The Emergency Repair Disk (ERD)

- Control Panel

The use of each of these options for troubleshooting purposes are covered in the following subsections.

Troubleshooting through the Event Viewer

The Event Viewer is used in NT to provide informational logs regarding your computer. Three different logs are kept; they are:

- System

- Security

- Application

These logs are defined in Table 6.4.

	Log	Description
T A B L E 6.4 Event Viewer Log Options	System	This log is used to provide information about the NT operating system. You can see information such as hardware failures, software configuration errors, and the general well-being of your computer
	Security	This log contains information related to auditing. If you choose to enable auditing, you will see success and/or failure events related to resources and processes based on enabled auditing
	Application	This log contains errors from applications that are running on your server. For example, SQL errors would be logged here

Within each log, events are recorded into one of five event categories; they are:

- Error
- Information
- Warning
- Success Audit
- Failure Audit

To access Event Viewer, select Start ➢ Programs ➢ Administrative Tools (Common) ➢ Event Viewer. Figure 6.1 shows an example of this screen.

By default, the oldest events will be at the bottom of the list and the newest events will be recorded at the top of the list. In the case of Figure 6.1, the bottom Stop message is related to NE2000. If you click on this entry, you will see more detailed information, as shown in Figure 6.2.

In this case the reported error specifies that the NE2000 adapter could not be found. It is important to identify the first error, because subsequent errors are often dependencies that will be corrected when you correct the initial problem.

Date	Time	Source	Category	Event	User
12/4/96	6:07:03 PM	BROWSER	None	8015	N/A
12/4/96	6:07:00 PM	BROWSER	None	8015	N/A
12/4/96	6:06:58 PM	BROWSER	None	8015	N/A
12/4/96	6:06:38 PM	DhcpServer	None	1024	N/A
12/4/96	6:05:22 PM	EventLog	None	6005	N/A
12/4/96	2:24:39 PM	Service Control Mar	None	7023	N/A
12/4/96	2:24:13 PM	DhcpServer	None	1008	N/A
12/4/96	2:24:13 PM	DhcpServer	None	1006	N/A
12/4/96	2:24:11 PM	Wins	None	4165	N/A
12/4/96	2:24:11 PM	Service Control Mar	None	7023	N/A
12/4/96	2:24:11 PM	Wins	None	4193	N/A
12/4/96	2:23:38 PM	EventLog	None	6005	N/A
12/4/96	2:23:40 PM	Service Control Mar	None	7000	N/A
12/4/96	2:23:40 PM	NE2000	None	5003	N/A
12/4/96	2:21:39 PM	BROWSER	None	8033	N/A

Event Viewer - System Log on \\INSTRUCTOR

Log View Options Help

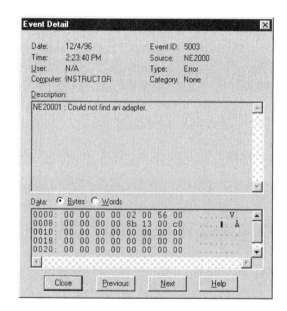

In this example, the NE2000 card has been configured incorrectly. To correct the problem, you would verify the NT settings through Control Panel ➤ Network ➤ Adapters ➤ Properties with the actual configuration on your network card.

Troubleshooting Using Server Manager

The Server Manager utility can also be used to identify configuration errors. Through Server Manager, you can identify which computers are currently active in the domain. This is often a first step to see if an NT client is active in the Domain. From there, troubleshooting can be focused toward application and service errors or network and protocol connectivity errors. In addition, for each computer you can see:

- The services running

- The users attached to the computer

- The resources being accessed

- The configuration of directory replication

If a service does not start automatically, you can manually try to start the service. If the service still doesn't start, you may receive an error message that can then be used to help track the problem.

Another good way to track configuration problems is through the Windows NT Diagnostics.

Troubleshooting Using Windows NT Diagnostics

The Windows NT Diagnostics utility can be very useful in diagnosing configuration errors. To access this utility, select Start ➢ Programs ➢ Administrative Tools (Common) ➢ Windows NT Diagnostics. You will see a screen similar to Figure 6.3.

An overview of each tab within the Windows NT Diagnostics main dialog box is provided in Table 6.5.

The next subsection describes the Last Known Good option and how it can be used to troubleshoot network configuration errors.

FIGURE 6.3

The Windows NT Diagnostics dialog box

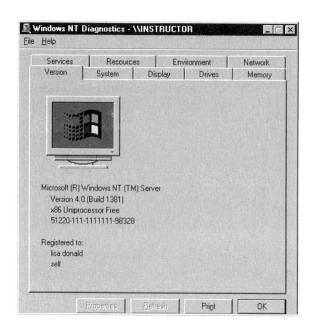

TABLE 6.5

Windows NT Diagnostics Tabs Defined

Windows NT Diagnostic Tab	Information Provided
Version	The Version tab shows the build of NT that you are using, including any service packs, the platform that NT is installed on, and the registration information
System	The System tab shows the platform that NT is installed on, the HAL (hardware abstraction layer) being used, BIOS information, and the identification of the processor(s) installed in the computer
Display	Display verbose information on your video adapter and driver
Drives	The Drives tab displays the drives that are currently detected. This includes floppy drives, local hard drives, and CD-ROM drives. If you click on a drive, you can see more detailed information. For example, you can see the number of clusters and the clusters in use and the attributes that are applied to the drive

TABLE 6.5 (cont.) Windows NT Diagnostics Tabs Defined	Windows NT Diagnostic Tab	Information Provided
	Memory	The Memory tab shows information on memory and memory usage. Includes information on physical RAM as well as the page file
	Services	The Services tab can provide a wealth of information. Two buttons allow you to select whether you want the services or devices. If you click Services, you can see all of services that are installed on your computer and the state of the service. If you click on a specific service, you see verbose information on the service including general information and service flags, as well as any dependencies the service has
	Resources	The Resources tab shows all of the resources that are in use on your computer. This is especially important when adding hardware because you can see what IRQs, I/O ports, DMA, and Memory addresses are in use. This can help identify conflicts between peripherals
	Environment	The Environment tab will show the environment variables that have been set for the system and the local user. You can see the variable and the value assigned to it
	Network	The Network tab shows general information such as the access levels of users who are logged on and the domains and servers that authenticated the users. In addition there are buttons for Transports, Settings, and Statistics, that allow you to see information as the tabs relate to the network

Troubleshooting with the Last Known Good Option

Each time you successfully log on, the system saves your configuration in the registry under HKEY_LOCAL_MACHINE\SYSTEM\CurrentControlSet. You can boot back to this configuration by selecting the Last Known Good configuration during system boot.

You could use this option if you changed your systems configuration, and it would no longer successfully boot.

An example would be upgrading your SCSI driver. The new driver is not correct and causes the NT boot to fail. By using the Last Known Good option, you would revert to your previous configuration with the driver that had previously worked.

The next subsection will overview the emergency repair disk.

During the boot process, you will see a screen asking you if you want to use the Last Known Good Configuration. If the answer is yes, press the space bar when you see this prompt.

Emergency Repair Disk (ERD)

The ERD is a repair disk which is created for each individual NT computer. It contains that computer's specific configuration information. The ERD contents include:

- Portions of the registry

- The computer's default profile

- The computer's configuration files

The following sections overview how to create the ERD and how to restore information from the ERD.

Creation of the ERD

To create the ERD, you take the following steps from the computer that the ERD is being created for.

1. Select Start ➤ Run.

2. In the Run dialog box, type **RDISK**.

3. Select the Create Repair Disk option.

4. Insert the floppy diskette and continue.

You can also run the RDISK program with the RDISK /s switch which saves all of the Registry information to the ERD. While this saves all Registry data, use this option with caution, as any changes to the Registry (local user accounts, passwords, and permissions) that are made after the last Repair Disk update will be overwritten if NT is recovered from the ERD.

That's all it takes to create the ERD. To restore the data from the ERD, see the next subsection.

Restoring Information from the ERD

If you need to use your ERD, you will need the three NT Setup diskettes. The ERD itself is not bootable, and most of the files are stored in compressed format.

To restore the ERD, you boot to the NT Setup Boot diskettes and choose the Repair option. You will be prompted for your unique ERD and will be asked to select what information (Registry files, NT System files, and so on) should be restored.

If you have misplaced your NT Setup Boot diskettes, you can create them by using the NT Server CD. From the I386 directory, type **WINNT /ox** (or **WINNT32 /ox** if you are on an NT platform).

Troubleshooting through Control Panel

You can also troubleshoot some configurations through Control Panel. One of the most commonly used Control Panel applets is the Network applet. Through Control Panel ➤ Network, you configure your identification, services, protocols, adapters, and bindings.

For each tab, you can view what is currently configured as well as re-configure options that are not correctly configured.

Unit 2 provides more detailed information on options that can be viewed and configured through Control Panel.

As you may have noticed, you almost always have to restart your NT computer after configuration changes are made.

The next section will highlight common print errors.

Troubleshooting Print Errors

Print errors have many causes. In order to troubleshoot a printer error, you should first try and isolate where the problem is occurring within the print process. The print process is composed of the following areas:

1. A shared printer is created on a print server by the administrator.

2. A client makes a connection to the shared printer.

3. The client application generates a print job and sends it to the shared printer.

4. The print server receives the job spools, and (possibly) renders (or processes) the job.

5. The print server directs the job to the print device.

6. The print device prints the job.

Some common print errors that you might encounter are listed in Table 6.6 along with possible solutions.

	Error	Possible Solution
TABLE 6.6 Common Print Problems and Solutions	The print job is printed as garbage, or prints with strange characters or fonts	Make sure the correct print driver is installed
	Hard disk is thrashing and print jobs are not being sent to the print device	Make sure that the disk has sufficient space—if not, move the spool file to another location
	Jobs are reaching the server and not printing, or are not reaching the print server	Stop and restart the spooler service

If you have jobs that have been submitted to a print device that is not functioning, you can create a new port on the print server and specify the UNC name of the failed printer. This allows the new print device to service existing jobs without users having to resubmit their print jobs.

To move the spooler file to another location, access the Advanced tab of the print server properties and specify an alternate spool file location. Spool files are defined for the print server as opposed to specific printers.

In the next section, you will learn about general RAS troubleshooting.

Troubleshooting RAS Errors

RAS errors can be caused by many things, but once RAS servers and clients are correctly established, errors are usually due to communication media quality, especially analog phone lines. This section will identify some of the more common problems caused by RAS hardware and RAS setup.

RAS Hardware

The following list of questions helps identify issues related to RAS hardware.

- Is the communication hardware on the HCL (hardware compatibility list)?
- If the hardware connects to a COM port, is the COM port enabled through system BIOS?
- If the hardware connects to a COM port, is the port good?
- Is the device configured correctly and not in conflict with any other system devices?
- Is the connection cable good and the proper type or configuration?

If you suspect that a modem is not working properly, you can edit the registry entry HKEY_LOCAL_MACHINE\System\CurrentControlSet\Services\ RasMan\Parameters and change the Logging entry to 1. This will enable a log called DEVICE.LOG to be created in the \WINNT\SYSTEM32\RAS folder. This log, which records all data that travels between the RAS Server, communication devices, and RAS Clients, can be used to diagnose modem connections.

Troubleshooting RAS Setup

If you know your hardware installation is good, then the next thing to check is the RAS configuration. You should try to narrow the problem to the RAS server or the RAS client. If other RAS clients can connect to the server or if the client can connect to other RAS servers, then you will have an idea of whether the problem is on the client or server side.

The following list identifies items to check in RAS setup:

- Ensure that the RAS Server service is running.

- Make sure that the user has RAS dial-in permissions. These permissions can be assigned through:

  - Remote Access Admin

  - User Manager for Domains

- Verify that the client is using PPP to connect to the RAS server.

- Make sure that the client and server are using a common protocol.

- Ensure that the client and server have a common encryption requirement.

To view the status of your RAS ports, you can use the Remote Access Admin utility.

The next section will help you identify connectivity problems.

Troubleshooting Connectivity Problems

Network connectivity problems can have many causes. Some network connectivity problems are related to hardware errors, while other problems are related to software. In this section, we'll address hardware problems first, then we'll address software-related problems.

Hardware Connectivity Errors

Some connectivity errors relate to hardware. Common errors that occur are:

- The adapter cable may be loose or bad.
- Your network card may be configured incorrectly.
- You network card may be bad.
- You may have a problem with other hardware such as a hub or cabling errors.

Generally, the first step in identifying a network connectivity error is to take the network cable from a computer that is working properly and attach it to the computer that is having problems. If a connection is established, you probably have a problem with the original cable—the cable is not connected, or maybe there is a problem with other network hardware. If no connection is established with the good cable, you may have a bad network card or it may be improperly configured.

Table 6.7 gives some possible solutions for each of these problems.

TABLE 6.7	Hardware Connectivity Error	Solution
Common Hardware Connectivity Problems and Solutions	Bad Jumper Cable	Test the connection with a known good cable. Make sure that you have the proper cable for the adapter card you are using. For example, if you are using 100 mbps Ethernet, make sure you have CAT5 twisted pair cable
	Incorrect Configuration on Network Card	Make sure the configuration on the NIC matched the configuration in NT. This is especially important for network cards that use software setup. If you are using Ethernet with multiple connectors, make sure that cable type is set properly

TABLE 6.7 (cont.) Common Hardware Connectivity Problems and Solutions	Hardware Connectivity Error	Solution
	Bad Network Card	This seems obvious, but some general tips are to make sure you don't handle the cards improperly. You may damage your card through ESD (electrostatic discharge). If you suspect the card is bad, test the card by replacing it with a known good card. This is rare unless you have had the workstation open or suffered an electrical system outage or surge
	Other Hardware Errors	Reset hubs if possible. Try and connect to a port that you know works

Remember to change only one component at a time when you troubleshoot.

The next subsection will help you identify software-related errors.

Software Connectivity Errors

If you have eliminated possible hardware errors, connectivity problems can also be related to software configuration errors. The first thing that you should verify is that the computers are running a common protocol. Once that has been verified, the following sections will provide information on troubleshooting NWLink and TCP/IP.

NWLink Errors

One of NWLinks advantages is that it is a simple protocol to install and configure. The main configuration error that occurs with NWLink is in configuring the frame type. Frame type refers to how data is formatted into frames for transmission. If the sender and receiver do not have matching frame types, they will not be able to communicate. This is especially important in Ethernet environments where there are four possible frame types to choose from. Different networking environments default to different frame types, as shown in Table 6.8.

	Frame Type	Environment Used In
T A B L E 6.8 Common Frame Type Usage	Ethernet_802.2	This is the IEEE Ethernet standard. NT will try and default to this frame type if you choose the auto-detect frame type. NetWare 3.12 and NetWare 4.x environments also use the Ethernet_802.2 frame type
	Ethernet_802.3	This is sometimes called Ethernet Raw because it does not have to use the 802.2 LLC header like the Ethernet_802.2 frame type does. This frame type was used by NetWare 3.11 and earlier
	Ethernet_II	This frame type used to be popular in UNIX environments using TCP/IP
	Ethernet_SNAP	Doesn't Apple always have to do things differently? This frame type is used by Macintoshes using EtherTalk adapters

As shown in Figure 6.4, when you select NWLink frame type, you can choose:

- Auto Frame Type Detection
- Manual Frame Type Detection

F I G U R E 6.4

The NWLink IPX/SPX Properties dialog box

In most cases, the Internal Network Number can be left at the default value of 00000000. Table 6.9 defines how you determine if you will use auto detect or manual configuration for frame type.

T A B L E 6.9 NWLink Frame Type Configuration Options	**Frame Type Option**	**When This Option Should Be Selected**
	Auto Frame Type Detection	You would use auto frame type detection if you weren't sure what frame type was being used and you wanted NT to auto detect what it found on the cable. NT will listen to the cable, and prefer the Ethernet_802.2 frame type. If Ethernet_802.2 cannot be detected, it will configure the first frame type it detects. Auto Frame Type only detects the first frame type it sees
	Manual Frame Type Detection	You mainly use manual frame type detection if you need to configure multiple frame types. For example, you will need to connect to a computer using Ethernet_802.2 and another computer running Ethernet_802.3. You would also use this option if your network used multiple frame types and you wanted to configure your computer for a frame type other than Ethernet_802.2

TCP/IP Errors

TCP/IP requires more configuration than NWLink, and is thus subject to more possible configuration errors. As seen in Figure 6.5, you can specify that TCP/IP be configured automatically through a DHCP server or manually.

Automatic TCP/IP Configuration   You can specify automatic configuration by specifying that you want to be a DHCP client. If there are errors with this configuration, you should check:

- That the DHCP server is operating and correctly configured (The easiest method is to verify that other clients can use DHCP.)

- That the physical media is good between the DHCP client and the DHCP server.

The Microsoft TCP/IP
Properties dialog box

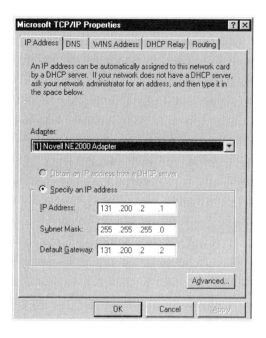

Manual TCP/IP Configuration   If you choose not to use DHCP, you can manually configure your TCP/IP client. The things to check are that you configured the IP address, subnet mask, and default gateway properly. Remember that only the IP address and subnet mask are required. A Default Gateway is needed only if routing out of the current workstation's subnet is desired. The next section defines additional utilities that can be used to troubleshoot TCP/IP.

Utilities Used to Identify TCP/IP Errors   TCP/IP comes with several utilities that can be used to troubleshoot TCP/IP. They are listed in Table 6.10.

T A B L E 6.10

TCP/IP Diagnostic
Utilities

TCP/IP Utility	Description
IPCONFIG	This is one of the most useful commands in diagnosing IP configuration errors. By using IPCONFIG, you will see your computers IP address, subnet mask, and default gateway. IPCONFIG /all will show more verbose IP configuration information. If you are using DHCP, you can use IPCONFIG /release and IPCONFIG /renew to drop and renew your DHCP configuration

TABLE 6.10 (cont.) TCP/IP Diagnostic Utilities	**TCP/IP Utility**	**Description**
	PING	Used to test a connection between two hosts by sending an ICMP echo request and echo reply. You can troubleshoot where an error is occurring by pinging the loopback address (127.0.0.1), the address of the local host, the default gateway, and the address of the remote host. If communications fail at any of these points, you have a better idea of where to look for the problem
	ARP	ARP is used to view the local ARP table which defines mappings between IP addresses and local hardware or MAC addresses
	NETSTAT	Used to show TCP/IP statistics and any current connections
	ROUTE, IPXROUTE	These commands are used to verify that all of the local routing tables are properly defined. ROUTE is used for TCP/IP routing while IPXROUTE is used for NWLink IPX/SPX routing
	TRACERT	This is a diagnostic utility that is used to trace the route of a packet across an internetwork. TRACERT works by sending an ICMP packet using echo request and echo reply

To help determine if the problem is protocol or hardware related, try installing NetBEUI. It is self-configuring and the most basic protocol. If you install Net-BEUI and are able to browse local resources, then you know that the hardware is good. This can be used as a litmus test for determining a NWLink IPX/SPX or TCP/IP software or configuration error versus a NIC error in the workstation or connection media error.

In the next section, you will learn how to troubleshoot resource access and permissions problems.

Troubleshooting Resource Access and Permission Problems

If you are having trouble accessing a resource, one common problem is that the account does not have the appropriate access permissions. The following subsections provide suggestions to help you troubleshoot access of local and network resources.

Local Access

If you are accessing a resource locally, you should determine if the resource is on a FAT or NTFS partition by selecting the Properties feature on the storage device that holds the resource.

- If the partition is FAT, then you know the problem does not relate to access permissions.

- If the partition is NTFS, the problem may be related to access permissions.

Figure 6.6 is used to illustrate some common access problems.

F I G U R E 6.6

An NTFS Permissions
Example

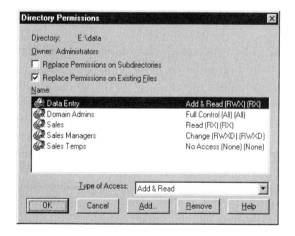

- Mary is a member of Sales and Sales Temps. Because Sales Temps has been assigned No Access, Mary will have No Access regardless of permissions she has been assigned through her membership in Sales.

- Michelle is a member of Sales. She tries to access E:\DATA\SUBDIR. When she tries to access the folder she is denied. When the administrator set up the permissions, the Replace Permissions on Subdirectories box was not checked.

- Tom has been a member of the Sales group. He was recently promoted to a manager and added to the Sales Managers group. However, when he accesses the E:\DATA folder, he can only Read data. Tom needs to log out and log on again to have his access token updated with his new membership.

Network Access

With network or remote access, you are governed by both share permissions and any NTFS permissions that may have been assigned. The more restrictive permission will be applied. The same issues that were involved with local access are also applied to network access.

Additionally, NTFS permission can implement file level permissions, but this is not recommended except for unique cases. An example of a unique case is if you had a folder that contained an application that contained an audit file. You could specify that the folder had Read permission, and all files in the folder would inherit Read permission. By specifying that the audit file had Change permission, the specific file permission would override the folders permissions.

Resolving Disk Failures in a Fault-Tolerant Environment

The main reason to implement fault tolerant disk strategies is so that when media hardware failure occurs, you do not lose mission critical data. In Unit 1, you learned how to select the appropriate fault tolerance solution. In this section, you will learn what to do when errors occur.

Tape Backup

No fault tolerance solution takes the place of tape backup. Tape backups are typically done daily. In the event of failure, you can always restore your data.

One backup solution is to use the NT Backup utility. This utility is used to back up and restore your NT server, including the Registry.

You should test your restore operation to verify your backups as good. This is part of any good disaster prevention strategy.

Disk Mirroring and Duplexing

Mirroring and duplexing are used to maintain duplicate copies of data on two separate drives. This is the only fault tolerance option available for the NT system and boot partition. It allows faster read and write access, but has 50% capacity drive storage. You handle mirror and duplex failures in the same manner.

Recovery options are based on whether or not the failed drive contains the boot partition. The following subsections describe recovery options of data drives and the boot partition drive.

Mirror Set Failure on a Data Drive

To recover from a mirror set failure on a data drive, you take the following steps:

1. Break the mirror set through Disk Administrator and delete the failed partition.

2. Replace the failed hard drive.

3. Use the Disk Administrator to establish a new mirror with the free space on the new drive.

Mirror Set Failure on the Boot Partition

If the boot partition is on a failed mirror set, you must determine if the primary drive failed, or the secondary drive failed. If the secondary drive failed, you would take the steps listed for recovery of a data drive.

If the primary drive failed, then recovery becomes more complex.

Prior to the failure, you should have created an NT boot floppy that contains an edited BOOT.INI file. This file should have the ARC location of the secondary drive. See Unit 1 for more information on ARC naming conventions. Then you would take the following steps:

1. Boot with the NT boot diskette you created prior to the failure.

2. Use Disk Administrator to break the mirror set and delete the failed partition.

3. Copy the BOOT.INI from the floppy disk to the system partition.

4. Replace the failed hardware.

5. Using the free space on the new drive, establish a new mirror set.

See the Troubleshooting Boot Failures section within this unit to identify which files should be copied to your NT boot diskette.

In the next subsection, you will learn how to recover from a disk failure if you are using a stripe set with parity.

Stripe Set with Parity

A stripe set with parity can contain 3–32 drives. If any of these drives fail, the data will be reconstructed from the parity information that is stored on the other drives within the stripe set. The system overhead in calculating the data from parity is very high, and you will notice significant performance degradation.

To regenerate your stripe set, you would take the following steps:

1. Replace the failed drive.

2. Use Disk Administrator to regenerate the stripe set using the free space on the new drive.

This concludes the troubleshooting overview. Now it's time to test your knowledge.

Troubleshooting Installation Errors

1. True or False. If your hardware works under other operating systems, it should work well with NT.

2. When you purchase hardware and components that will be used with NT, you should make sure the hardware is on the _____.

3. True or False. During the installation phase on NT Server, you can join a domain if the PDC is down, as long as at least one BDC for the domain is running.

4. What procedure should you take if your NT server is blue screening during installation because you are using a new SCSI adapter and NT does not have the driver so the SCSI driver is not being properly identified?

_____

5. Before you install NT, you should make sure that all of your components are properly installed and configured. When installing the components what three areas of configuration (besides IRQ) should you check so that you know there is no overlap in configuration.

_____

_____

_____

Troubleshooting Boot Failures

6.   You receive an error message stating:

> Windows NT could not start because the following file is missing or
> corrupt:
> \winnt\system32\ntoskrnl.exe
> Please re-install a copy of the above file.

What two boot files would cause this message to be generated?

_____

_____

7.   The _____ boot file is used to control the boot
process.

8.   If you were booting NT and discovered that any of the boot files were missing or corrupt, what would be the easiest way to restore the files?

_____

9.   The _____ boot file is used to build the boot menu choices, as well as to point to the location of the boot partition through an ARC name.

10.   What file is used to load an alternate operating system during the NY boot process?

_____

11.   What NT boot file is used to detect any hardware that has been installed and add that information to the system registry?

_____

12. The _____ boot file is used to load the NT kernel.

13. You receive the following error message:

```
I\0 error accessing boot sector file
multi(0)disk(0)rdisk(0)partition(1): \bootsect.dos
```

What missing or corrupt file would generate this error?

14. Your hardware configuration includes an SCSI adapter that does not use any BIOS settings. What additional boot file will be required?

Troubleshooting Configuration Errors

15. What utility provides information on any messages that are generated on NT computers?

16. You want to confirm all of the IRQs, base memory addresses, i/o memory addresses, and DMA channels that are in use on your computer. What utility do you use?

17. You are using the Event Viewer to view all of the messages that have been generated by your SQL server. What log do you use?

18.   How do you boot to the Last Known Good configuration?

_____

19.   What command is used to generate the emergency repair disk?

_____

20.   True or False. The ERD is a bootable disk.

21.   List the three logs that are generated through the Event Viewer.

_____

_____

_____

22.   True or False. When you use the Event Viewer and see that multiple errors are occurring, the last error usually indicates the source of the errors.

23.   What utility would you use to all of the NT computers that were active in the domain, and the type of operating system each computer was using?

_____

24.   If you suspected that a network protocol was incorrectly configured, what utility would you use?

_____

25. True or False. The ERD is a unique disk to each NT computer and should not be shared with other NT computers.

26. You would use the _____ utility if you wanted to see what version of NT you were running, and if any service packs had been applied.

27. The _____ utility is used to view the services that are running on the local as well as remote computers. You can also start, stop, pause, and restart services from this utility.

Troubleshooting Printer Errors

28. If you had just installed a new printer and the test page printed garbage, what would be the most likely problem?

_____

29. If your print jobs were reaching the server and not printing, or if your print jobs could not make it to the print server, what is the first course of action you should take?

_____

30. You are sending large graphics jobs to a network printer. Due to the size and nature of your print jobs, your print spooler runs out of disk space. How do you specify an alternate print spooler location?

_____

31. If you had a network print device that failed, and you wanted to re-direct the print jobs to another print device, what steps would you take?

Troubleshooting RAS Errors

32. Your RAS client is having problems connecting to the RAS server. You suspect that the correct WAN protocol is not being used. What WAN protocol must be used by RAS clients in order to connect to an NT server running the RAS server software?

33. You have RAS clients that are running UNIX as their client platform. When they dial-in to your RAS server they can't connect. You suspect the encryption on the server may be a problem since the UNIX clients have no encryption support. What encryption setting should you verify on the RAS server?

34. You suspect that the RAS modems you are using are causing RAS connection problems. How do you enable the DEVICE.LOG log file?

35. You have enabled the DEVICE.LOG log file for RAS troubleshooting. What will be the default location of this file?

36. You are dialing in as a RAS client and receive an error message indicating that you do not have RAS dial-in permissions. What two utilities can the administrator use to allow you access permissions?

_____

_____

37. The _____ utility can be used to view the status of your RAS ports.

Troubleshooting Connectivity Problems

38. What is the most common configuration error related to the NWLink IPX/SPX compatible transport protocol?

_____

39. What are the four Ethernet frame types associated with NWLink IPX/SPX compatible transport protocol?

_____

_____

_____

_____

40. When manually configuring TCP/IP what three options must be configured correctly?

_____

_____

_____

41. The _____ command can be used to test an IP connection between two hosts by sending an ICMP echo request and hopefully receiving an ICMP echo reply.

42. The _____ diagnostic utility is used with TCP/IP to trace the routes of packets through an internetwork. This command uses ICMP packets.

43. The _____ command can be used to see your current IP configuration including your IP address, subnet mask, and default gateway.

Troubleshooting Resource Access and Permission Problems

44. If a folder has both NTFS and share permissions applied, and a local user accesses the resource, what permissions will be applied?

_____

45. If a folder has both NTFS and share permissions applied, and a network user accesses the resource, what permissions will be applied?

_____

46. Rick is a member of the Sales Users, Sales Temps, and Sales Managers groups. The Sales folder has the following permissions assigned:

Sales Users: Read

Sales Temps: No Access

Sales Managers: Change

What are Rick's access permissions to the Sales folder?

47. The Engineering folder has the following NTFS permissions assigned:

Engineers: Read

Engineering Managers: Full Control

Kevin has been a member of Engineers since he started work at the company. Today he was promoted to a managerial position and added to the Engineering Managers group. When he tries to access the Engineering folder, he can only read data and execute files. What is the most likely problem?

48. You have a folder called Acct that contains a subfolder called 1997 and a subfolder called 1998. The Acct folder has the following permissions applied:

Sales Users:Read

Sales Managers:Change

Steve is a member of the Sales Users group. When he accesses the Acct folder he can only read. When he accesses the \Acct\1997 or \Acct\1998 folders, he has Full Access. What is the most likely cause of his addition access permissions?

Resolving Disk Failures in a Fault-Tolerant Environment

49. Your mirror set fails on the boot partition. What is more labor intensive to recover, a failure on the primary partition or a failure on the secondary partition?

_____

50. What are the steps you would take to recover from a single disk failure if you are using disk striping with parity?

_____

51. What are the steps you would take if you needed to recover from two disks failing in your stripe set with parity?

_____

52. What steps would be required if a mirror set only containing data suffered a disk failure?

_____

53. What steps would be required if your mirror set containing the boot partition failed, and the primary drive was the failure?

_____

54. Your entire registry is corrupt. What utility should be used to backup and restore the entire registry?

_____

55. What file should be edited for the NT boot floppy that is created for the mirror partition containing the boot partition and will be used in the event of primary disk failure?

_____

S A M P L E   T E S T

6-1   You are running NT Server. The server has been functioning correctly for several months. However, when you restarted the computer this morning, you received the following error message:

```
Windows NT could not start because the following file is missing or corrupt:

\winnt\system32\ntoskrnl.exe.

Please re-install a copy of the above file.
```

The only thing that changes between the last successful boot and the unsuccessful boot is that you used Disk Administrator to add a new partition to your hard drive. What file should you suspect as the problem?

   A. NTLDR

   B. NTDETECT.COM

   C. NTOSKRNL.EXE

   D. BOOT.INI

6-2   You have chosen to use disk striping with parity as your fault tolerance configuration on your NT server. Everything is running smoothly until one of your drives in the stripe set fails. After the drive fails, you notice that your system performance has dropped dramatically. How do you fix the problem?

   A. Replace the failed hardware, use the Disk Administrator utility to regenerate the stripe set with parity.

   B. Break the stripe set, replace the failed hardware, use the Disk Administrator utility to regenerate a new stripe set with parity.

   C. Replace the failed hardware, boot to the Last Known Good option, then use the Disk Administrator utility to regenerate the stripe set with parity.

   D. Replace the failed hardware, boot the system with the NT Setup Disks, use the Repair option with the ERD and then use Disk Administrator to regenerate the stripe set with parity.

SAMPLE TEST

6-3   Your NT system partition was attacked by a virus. Now all of your boot files are corrupt, and need to be replaced. What do you do?

    A. Put the ERD in your floppy drive and from A: type **ERD /s**.

    B. Put the ERD in your floppy drive and from A: type **RDISK /s**.

    C. Boot from the NT Setup boot floppies, choose the repair option, then use your ERD to verify and restore the NT system files.

    D. Boot NT and use the Last Known Good option.

6-4   Your company is a manufacturer of SCSI adapters. So naturally, you have installed your companies adapter in your NT server. The driver that you have used for the adapter is very stable. However, your R&D department has been working on a new driver that will offer significant enhancements. You install the new driver and now your NT server will no longer boot properly. What do you do?

    A. Put the ERD in your floppy drive and from A: type **ERD /s**.

    B. Put the ERD in your floppy drive and from A: type **RDISK /s**.

    C. Boot from the ERD to verify and restore the NT configuration.

    D. Boot NT and use the Last Known Good option.

6-5   Your company uses an NT network. You have installed and configured several print servers and network printers for your users. One of the print servers is not working correctly. Users send their jobs, but for some reason, they are not printing properly. What course of action should you take?

    A. Delete the printer that is causing problems, re-create the printer, ask the users to resubmit their print jobs.

    B. Delete the print server that is causing problems, re-create the print server, recreate the shared printer, and ask the users to resubmit their print jobs.

    C. Stop the spooler service and then restart the spooler service.

    D. Stop the print server service and then restart the print server service.

SAMPLE TEST

6-6   You are using RAS to provide dial-in connectivity for your remote users. You suspect that one of your modems is not working properly and you want to enable logging so that you can better troubleshoot the problem. How do you enable device logging?

    A. Use the RAS Administrator and from the Advanced tab, check the Enable the `DEVICE.LOG` file option.

    B. From Control Panel ➢ Network ➢ Services ➢ Remote Access Server ➢ Properties, check the Advanced tab and check the Enable Logging option.

    C. Edit the registry entry `HKEY_LOCAL_MACHINE\System\CurrentControlSet\ Services\RASMAN\Parameters\Logging` and specify value 1 to enable logging.

    D. From Control Panel ➢ Network ➢ Services ➢ Remote Access Server ➢ Properties, check the Logging tab and check the Enable Logging option.

6-7   Your network uses a mixture of NT and NetWare servers. For compatibility, you have standardized on the NWLink IPX/SPX compatible transport on your NT computers. One of your NT servers acts as a gateway to the NetWare servers and is running GSNW. A user is sitting at the NT server and tries to access NetWare resources. The user can see some NetWare servers, but cannot see other NetWare servers. What is the most likely problem?

    A. Some of the NetWare servers have not been configured with a NetWare gateway account for GSNW to use.

    B. The user account that is trying to access the NetWare resources does not have access permissions to the NetWare servers.

    C. You have not configured the default gateway property in the NWLink IPX/SPX compatible transport properly.

    D. The servers that you can see are using the same NWLink frame type that the NT server is configured with and the servers you don't see are using a different frame type. You should use manual configuration and select multiple frame types to match what all servers on the network are using.

SAMPLE TEST

6-8   Your network uses the TCP/IP protocol as its transport protocol. You use DHCP to assign the networks IP addresses automatically. You've been having problems with a shortage of IP addresses and over the weekend, expanded the scope of your DHCP server. You realize Monday morning that you set the scope improperly. You re-configure the DHCP server. While the server was misconfigured, some DHCP clients received IP configuration from the DHCP server. What command do you use to force the clients to drop the DHCP configuration information?

A. DHCP /release

B. DHCP /drop

C. IPCONFIG /release

D. IPCONFIG /drop

6-9   Traci is a user on your NT domain. She currently belongs to the Domain Users, Accounting Users, and Accounting Managers group. Traci is trying to access a share called ACCOUNTING on the ACCTSERVER computer. The permissions on the share allow the group Everyone Full Control. However, the folder the share is located on is NTFS and has the following permissions applied.

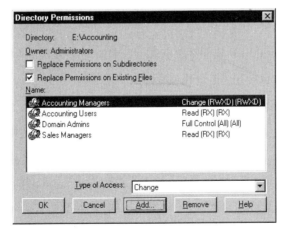

What will Traci's access permissions be over the share?

A. No Access

B. Read

C. Change

D. Full Control

6-10 Wendy is a user on your NT domain. She currently belongs to the Domain Users, Accounting Users, Accounting Managers, and Accounting Temps. She needs access to a share called ACCOUNTING on the ACCTSERVER computer. The permissions on the share allow the group Everyone Full Control. However, the folder the share is located on is NTFS and has the following permissions applied.

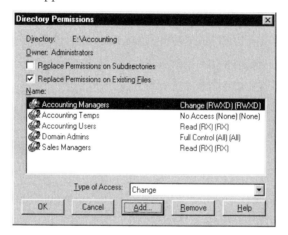

What will Wendy's access permissions be over the share?

A. No Access

B. Read

C. Change

D. Full Control

6-11 You have installed NT server using disk striping with parity as your fault tolerance configuration. You have 32 drives installed in the stripe set. Over the weekend two of the drives in the stripe set fail. What do you need to do to recover from the failure?

   A. Replace the failed hardware, use the Disk Administrator utility to regenerate the stripe set with parity.

   B. Break the stripe set, replace the failed hardware, use the Disk Administrator utility to regenerate a new stripe set with parity, then restore the data from tape backup.

   C. Replace the failed hardware, boot to the Last Known Good option, then use the Disk Administrator utility to regenerate the stripe set with parity.

   D. Replace the failed hardware, boot the system with the NT Setup Disks, use the Repair option with the ERD and then use Disk Administrator to regenerate the stripe set with parity.

6-12 You inherited your NT network from an administrator who has since left the company. One of the problems that you are facing is that you have no idea where any of the software or documentation that relates to your network is. One of the first things you did when you took over the position was to create ERDs for each NT computer. This was a good move, because you now need to use one of the ERDs you created. The problem is that you can find the NT Server CD, but you can't find the three NT Setup Boot disks. What is the quickest way to re-create the setup boot disks?

   A. Visit the Microsoft Web site. You can download the files you need.

   B. From a computer running NT, use the NT Server CD and from the I386 directory type: `WINNT32 /ox`.

   C. From a computer running DOS, use the NT Server CD and from the I386 directory type: `WINNT32 /ox`.

   D. From a computer running NT, use the NT Server CD and from the I386 directory type: `WINNT32 /bootd`.

6-13   You are running NT Server on your computer. During the boot process, you are asked what you want to boot to. You can choose from NT Server, NT Server (vga mode), or MS-DOS. You choose to boot to MS-DOS and your computer hangs. What file is most likely missing or corrupt?

   A. NTLDR

   B. BOOT.INI

   C. BOOTSECT.DOS

   D. MSDOS.SYS

6-14   You have installed NT server using disk mirroring your fault tolerance configuration. Your mirror set includes the system and boot partition. The secondary drive in the mirror set fails. What do you need to do to recover from the failure?

   A. Break the mirror set through Disk Administrator, replace the failed hardware, use Disk Administrator to establish a new mirror using the free space on the new hard drive.

   B. Break the mirror set, replace the failed hardware, use the Disk Administrator utility to regenerate the mirror set.

   C. Replace the failed hardware, boot to the Last Known Good option, then use the Disk Administrator utility to regenerate the mirror set.

   D. Boot the system with the NT setup boot disk that contains an edited BOOT.INI, break the mirror set in Disk Administrator, copy the BOOT.INI file to the system partition, replace the failed hardware, and then using the free space on the new hard drive, establish a new mirror set.

6-15 You have installed NT server using disk mirroring your fault tolerance configuration. Your mirror set includes the system and boot partition. The primary drive in the mirror set fails. What do you need to do to recover from the failure?

A. Break the mirror set through Disk Administrator, replace the failed hardware, use Disk Administrator to establish a new mirror using the free space on the new hard drive.

B. Break the mirror set, replace the failed hardware, use the Disk Administrator utility to regenerate the mirror set.

C. Replace the failed hardware, boot to the Last Known Good option, then use the Disk Administrator utility to regenerate the mirror set.

D. Boot the system with the NT boot disk that contains an edited BOOT.INI, break the mirror set in Disk Administrator, copy the BOOT.INI file to the system partition, replace the failed hardware, and then using the free space on the new hard drive, establish a new mirror set.

6-16 When you boot your NT server, you receive an error message letting you know that one or more services have failed to start. Furthermore, the error message tells you that you should check the Event Viewer. You check Event View and see the following log. Which error represents the most serious error?

Event Viewer - System Log on \\INSTRUCTOR					
Log View Options Help					
Date	**Time**	**Source**	**Category**	**Event**	**User**
12/4/96	6:07:03 PM	BROWSER	None	8015	N/A
12/4/96	6:07:00 PM	BROWSER	None	8015	N/A
12/4/96	6:06:58 PM	BROWSER	None	8015	N/A
12/4/96	6:06:38 PM	DhcpServer	None	1024	N/A
12/4/96	6:05:22 PM	EventLog	None	6005	N/A
12/4/96	2:24:39 PM	Service Control Mar	None	7023	N/A
12/4/96	2:24:13 PM	DhcpServer	None	1008	N/A
12/4/96	2:24:13 PM	DhcpServer	None	1006	N/A
12/4/96	2:24:11 PM	Wins	None	4165	N/A
12/4/96	2:24:11 PM	Service Control Mar	None	7023	N/A
12/4/96	2:24:11 PM	Wins	None	4193	N/A
12/4/96	2:23:38 PM	EventLog	None	6005	N/A
12/4/96	2:23:40 PM	Service Control Mar	None	7000	N/A
12/4/96	2:23:40 PM	NE2000	None	5003	N/A
12/4/96	2:21:39 PM	BROWSER	None	8033	N/A

   A. Browser

   B. Event Log

   C. Service Control Manager

   D. NE2000

6-17   Your NT network consists of a PDC, three BDCs and 500 NT Workstations. One of the users on an NT workstation calls and complains that their Virus Scanner keeps causing weird error messages. You suspect the problem is caused by some re-configuration that was done to the virus scanner. You are sitting at your NT workstation that has the administrative tools installed. The first thing you want to do is stop the scanner service and restart the service. What utility do you use?

   A. Server Manager

   B. Windows NT Diagnostics

   C. Control Panel ➤ Services

   D. Windows NT Explorer

6-18   Your network segment has become overloaded due to an increase in multi-media applications that your users are using over the network. You decide to add a second network adapter to your NT server so that you can subnet tour network into two network segments. What utility can you use to identify what devices are already installed and what configurations they are using so that you can make sure that your new network card is configured uniquely?

   A. Server Manager

   B. Windows NT Diagnostics

   C. Control Panel ➤ Services

   D. Windows NT Explorer

SAMPLE TEST

6-19 Jim is a user in the Accounting department. He needs to be able to access the Accounting folder with Change permissions so that he can update accounting information. Jim belongs to the Accounting Users group, and you have just added him to the Accounting Managers group. The NTFS permissions assigned to the folder are:

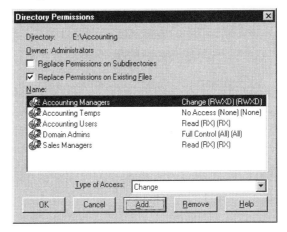

When Jim tries to access the Accounting folder, he only has Read access. What action should be taken?

A. Jim needs to log out and log on again so that his access token will be updated to reflect his new group membership.

B. You need to close the Accounting folder and re-open the Accounting folder so that the new permissions will be applied.

C. You need to shutdown the computer that contains the Accounting folder and restart the computer so that changes will take effect.

D. Jim needs to shut down his computer and restart it so that the changes will take effect.

6-20   You have just installed a new printer. When the printer tries to send a test page the printer spews out a ton of paper with strange symbols. What is the most likely problem?

    A. The print server does not have enough disk space to support the spool file.

    B. You used an incorrect print driver.

    C. You configured the printer on the wrong port.

    D. The printer was configured with the wrong protocol or the protocol is mis-configured.

6-21   Your network print device services about 25 users. The print device is used fairly heavily and always has print jobs waiting in the spool file. After much use, the printer dies. During the troubleshooting phase you discover that the power supply has died. It will take a week to get the printer fixed. In the meantime, you have a spare printer that you will use. How do you configure the new printer so that is receives all the jobs that were directed to the broken printer?

    A. Create a new printer, give it the same name as the old printer.

    B. Create a new printer, use the cut and copy procedure to cut the jobs from the broken printer and paste them to the new printer. Direct users to send new jobs to the new printers name.

    C. Create a new printer. Delete the jobs from the old printer. Have users resubmit old jobs and send new jobs to the new printers name.

    D. Add a port to the failed print server, then specify the UNC of the failed printer. This will automatically redirect print jobs from the failed printer and allow users to continue sending jobs using their current configuration. They will only need to be told to pick up their jobs from a different print device.

SAMPLE TEST

6-22   Your company manufacturers SCSI adapters. You decide to install NT Server on a computer that is using an SCSI adapter that has just come out. NT does not have a driver for the SCSI adapter and during the installation phase, keeps blue screening. What is the easiest solution for your problem?

    A. When NT goes to recognize your mass storage devices, press S to specify an additional device, then provide the diskette that contains your SCSI adapters NT driver.

    B. When NT goes to recognize your mass storage devices, press the manual configuration button and provide the diskette that contains your SCSI adapters NT driver.

    C. Copy the contents of the I386 directory to your hard drive, then copy the driver for your SCSI adapter. Run WINNT from the command line. If NTDETECT can find your SCSI driver, it will automatically load the correct driver.

    D. Install an SCSI adapter that has an NT driver. Install NT. Add your SCSI adapter and from Control Panel ➤ Devices, specify the new device and provide the driver when prompted.

6-23   You have installed disk mirroring on your system and boot partition for fault tolerance. You test the boot disk, and find that you cannot boot from it. Your configuration includes a SCSI adapter without the BIOS enabled. You remember reading that this configuration requires an extra boot file. What is the required file?

    A. NTLDR

    B. BOOT.SYS

    C. SCSI.SYS

    D. NTBOOTDD.SYS

6-24   You are very concerned with fault tolerance. You decide to update the emergency repair disk for all of the NT computers on your network. What command or utility do you use? Choose all that apply.

    A. ERD

    B. RDISK

    C. Disk Administrator

    D. Server Manager

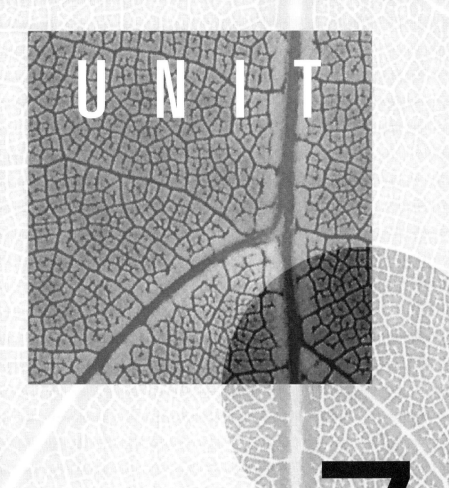

UNIT

7

Final Review

$\mathbf{T}$hink you're ready for the exam yet? Here's a good way to find out. Grab your watch and take note of the time. The real exam will have 55 questions with a 90-minute time limit. Here are 55 questions. Get ready, get set, GO!

1 You installed a network printer at the print server. Your users are sending large graphics files to the printer and are having problems printing because the spool file keeps filling up. You install a new hard drive on the print server and configure it and format it to be NTFS. How do you configure the print server to use the alternate spool file?

    A. From the Printers Control Panel dialog box choose Server Properties ➤ Advanced tab.

    B. From the Printers Control Panel dialog box choose Advanced Print Server Properties.

    C. From the Printers Control Panel dialog box choose Server Properties ➤ Spooler Properties.

    D. You can only configure this through editing the Registry with REGEDIT or REGEDT32.

2 You have a dual-language HP printer that switches between PCL and PostScript printing. You want to make sure that the printer can switch modes correctly. What is the best way to manage this?

    A. Create two printers, one called PCL and one called PostScript. Advise users to send their jobs to the appropriate printer.

    B. Make sure that you are using the HP network print monitor, `Hpmon.dll`.

    C. Use separator files.

    D. The printer will automatically switch back and forth and this never causes problems.

3   You have configured your NT server's hard drive so that you have two partitions. A 20MB FAT partition, C:\, and a 1GB NTFS partition, D. The system is configured so that the only files on the C:\ are the files needed to boot NT. A disgruntled employee tried to sabotage your server and managed to format the C:\ drive before he was caught. No other damage was done, but now NT can't boot. What should you do to recover from this situation?

   A. Call 911.

   B. Boot from ERD and specify that you want your boot files fixed.

   C. Boot from the three setup floppies and use the repair option with your ERD to fix the boot files.

   D. Format a floppy on another NT server using NTFS. Copy the boot files over, then boot with the floppy you have just created.

   E. Boot to DOS, place your ERD in the floppy drive, and use the ERD.EXE command.

4   Your NT server has recently had several new applications added. After the applications were installed, you noticed that the percentage of free disk space was very low. So, you have just installed a new hard drive on your NT server. You want this drive to use the NTFS format. You use Disk Administrator and create the parition, but the Format option is greyed out. Why?

   A. You are not logged in as a user with adminitrative rights.

   B. You must commit the changes first.

   C. You must mark the drive as active.

   D. You probably created an extended partition, and you have to assign drive space and a drive letter to the partition before it can be formatted.

FINAL REVIEW

5 You are running an NT server that has a 2GB drive that is partitioned and formatted with FAT. You want to install Services for Macintosh and share files on this server with Macs. In order to accomplish this, your partition needs to be NTFS. You are scared that you might lose existing data. You make a backup. Which method will require the least amount of effort from you to make this partition NTFS without having to use your tape backup?

    A. Use Disk Administrator ➤ Tools ➤ Convert.

    B. Use My Computer, then select your drive. Choose Properties ➤ Convert.

    C. Use the `CONVERT` command line utility.

    D. Use the `FORMAT` command line utility and specify the `/fs:ntfs` switch.

6 Your computer was originally configured with DOS. When you installed NT, you noticed that you had three options on your boot loader menu. You could boot to NT Server, NT Server VGA mode, or DOS. You've successfully booted to DOS before. Now everything works when you boot to NT, but your computer will not boot to DOS. Which file should you check?

    A. `DOS.SYS`

    B. `BOOTDOS.SYS`

    C. `BOOTSECT.DOS`

    D. `BOOTSYS.DOS`

7 You are configuring a boot floppy that can be used to boot NT in a troubleshooting scenario. Which boot file is required if you are booting NT using an SCSI controller with the BIOS disabled?

    A. `SCSIBOOT.SYS`

    B. `NTBOOTDD.SYS`

    C. `BOOTSCSI.SYS`

    D. `NTSCSI.SYS`

8   You have noticed that when you boot NT, you get a selection screen that shows that you can boot to NT Server, NT Server VGA mode, and DOS. You have read that you can edit the file that contains this information. You want to add a new selection that will give you verbose boot information by adding the switch /SOS to a new line in the boot file. Which file contains the information that is used to build the boot loader screen?

    A. NTLDR

    B. NTOSKRNL.EXE

    C. BOOT.INI

    D. NTDETECT.COM

9   You are very concerned with fault tolerance. You use a third party utility that backs up your data on a daily basis. However, the backup utility you use will not backup the NT registry. Which utility should you use to get a complete backup of your server's registry?

    A. Use the NT Backup program.

    B. From REGEDT32, choose Tools ➤ Backup Registry.

    C. Use the ERD command; this will create an emergency repair disk that contains your entire registry.

    D. Use the RDISK command, this will create an emergency repair disk that contains the entire registry.

10   You are using the NT Backup utility on your PDC. You back up 4 NT servers and 30 NT workstations. Everything worked well until you added 10 new workstations. With the new workstations it takes until 9:30 in the morning to complete your backups. You want your backups to finish before 7:00 in the morning. What should you do?

    A. Add another tape drive to your PDC and specify that you want half the machines to back up to the first drive and half the machines to back up to the second drive.

    B. Add a tape carousel to your PDC to increase tape capacity, while still keeping everything automated.

C. Purchase another tape backup unit and install it onto another server, specify that half of the computers back up to the PDC and half of the computers back up to the new backup unit.

D. Use RAID 5 on the servers; then you should only have to back up the workstations, freeing up space on your tape backup unit.

11 Your NT server has a single IDE drive that will contain the system and boot partition. You also have five SCSI drives that are 850MB each. You want the best combination of speed, fault tolerance, and maximized data storage. Which disk configuration should you choose?

A. Disk mirroring

B. Disk duplexing

C. Disk striping

D. Disk striping with parity

12 You are concerned with disk performance and have decided to implement disk striping. What is the minimum hardware you need to implement disk striping?

A. One controller, two drives

B. Two controllers, two drives

C. One controller, three drives

D. One controller, four drives

13 You have chosen the disk striping with parity disk configuration. What is the minimum hardware you need to implement disk striping with parity?

A. One controller, two drives

B. Two controllers, two drives

C. One controller, three drives

D. One controller, four drives

14   You have three NT member servers in your domain. You and another IS employee are responsible for managing the servers. They are in a locked room that you don't visit on a daily basis. The problem is that occasionally the servers generate error messages that you need to know about right away. Which utility can you use to send the error messages to you and your partner in crime, no matter which computer you are logged in to?

    A. Event Viewer ➤ Tools

    B. Server Manager

    C. Performance Manager

    D. User Manager for Domains

15   You have a NetWare server that you want to replace with an NT server. The NetWare server has data on it that you want to copy to the NT server. You decide to use Migration Tool for NetWare. What is the pre-requisite software that must be loaded on the NT server?

    A. RIP for IPX

    B. RIP for NWLink IPX/SPX

    C. CSNW

    D. GSNW

16   You are using Performance Monitor and notice that you have a very high disk I/O due to excessive paging. What is the best solution to this problem?

    A. Get a faster disk I/O channel.

    B. Spread the paging file over multiple physical disk channels.

    C. Increase the size of the paging file.

    D. Add more RAM to the computer.

17 You are very concerned with fault tolerance. You implement disk duplexing in your data drives on your NT server. Over the weekend the primary drive in the mirrored set fails. What is the first step on your road to recovery?

  A. Replace the failed drive.

  B. Break the duplex set in Disk Administrator.

  C. Break the mirror set in Disk Administrator.

  D. Break the mirror set in Server Manager.

18 You have a C:\ drive that's a FAT partition and a D:\ drive that's an NTFS partition. What will happen to the file permissions and long file name information if you copy files from D:\ to C:\? Select two answers.

  A. The files will still have long file names.

  B. The file names will be truncated to 8.3 naming convention.

  C. The file permissions will be copied.

  D. The file permissions will not be copied.

19 You have a C:\ drive that's an NTFS partition and a D:\ drive that's an NTFS partition. What will happen to the file permissions and attributes if you copy files from D:\ to C:\? Select two answers.

  A. The file attributes will be copied from the source directory.

  B. New file attributes will be inherited from the destination directory.

  C. The file permissions will be copied from the source directory.

  D. The file permissions will be inherited from the destination directory.

20   You have a D:\ drive that's an NTFS partition. What will happen to the file permissions and attributes if you move a file from D:\ACCT to D:\SALES? Select two answers.

    A. The attributes will be copied from the source directory.

    B. New file attributes will be inherited from the destination directory.

    C. The file permissions will be copied from the source directory.

    D. The file permissions will be inherited from the destination directory.

21   Your domain consists of one PDC and three BDCs. The PDC stores all of the information for the users logon scripts and the system policies for the domain. You need this information copied to the BDCs, so you are using directory replication. What is the default directory that the import computers will use?

    A. \WINNT\SYSTEM32\REPL\IMPORT

    B. \WINNT\REPL\IMPORT

    C. \REPL\IMPORT\SCRIPTS

    D. \NETLOGON

22   Your C:\ contains your system and boot partition. You are concerned that if this drive fails, you will have significant down time, possibly during production hours. You want to implement fault tolerance on this partition. Which of the following options can you use? Choose all that apply.

    A. Disk striping

    B. Disk mirroring

    C. Disk duplexing

    D. Disk striping with parity

23   You have noticed that over the last year your NT servers performance has seemed to slow down. You decide that you want to start tracking performance on a regular basis so that you can see if the server is performing at the same level, or if it's just your imagination. So, you want to create a baseline for your NT server using Performance Monitor. You will be tracking counters for your computer over a 48-hour period. Which view should you use during the configuration process?

A. Chart

B. Log

C. Report

D. Alert

24   You have recently configured Performance Monitor for your NT server. You configured counters for processor, memory, disk, and network access. After you run Performance Monitor for a week you notice that all of the counters that track disk statistics are flat. What steps should you take?

A. Run DISKPERF -y.

B. Run DISKCOUNT -y.

C. Start the DISKPERF service.

D. Restart your computer.

25   You have 20 sales users who spend about half their time in the office and half their time on the road. Since the users are never in the office at the same time, you only have 12 cubicles for these users. When the sales users are in the office, they sit at any available desk. Currently users configurations are not available from one computer to another. You decide to implement roaming profiles. How do you create a roaming profile?

A. Through System Profile Editor.

B. Through System Profile Manager.

C. Through Control Panel > System > Profiles tab.

D. By specifying a UNC path in User Manager for Domains User Profiles box.

26   You have three separate drives. You want to maximize the paging file. What action(s) should you take?

    A. Place the paging file on the same partition as the system partition.

    B. Place the paging file on the same partition as the boot partition.

    C. Place the paging file on multiple logical drives.

    D. Place the paging file on multiple physical drives.

27   When you installed your domain, you installed a PDC and three member servers. Your PDC crashed briefly last week causing chaos. You want to make sure this doesn't happen again. What is the best solution?

    A. Copy the SAM database to one of the member servers.

    B. Promote a member server to BDC through Server Manager.

    C. Define one of the member servers as a BDC through Control Panel > Network > Identification tab.

    D. Back up a member server, install it as a BDC, restore the data to the new BDC.

28   You have decided to implement a printer pool for the secretarial pool in a large law firm. Currently the secretaries all sit in the same location and use six different printers. Which of the following is a requirement to implement a printing pool for these printers?

    A. The printer devices must be the same model.

    B. The printer devices must use the same print driver.

    C. The printer devices must be attached to the same print server.

    D. The print devices must all use the same printer port.

29   Your company uses a mixture of NetWare and NT servers. You use the NWLink protocol to pro-
      vide connectivity to the NetWare servers. You can see some of the servers, but you can't see other
      servers. What is the most common configuration error associated with NWLink?

      A. IPX address

      B. Subnet mask

      C. Frame type

      D. Default gateway

30   Last month, your NT server ran out of disk space just as the VP for you department was trying to
      save a Word document he had been working on for hours. You were in hot water. You want to
      make sure that this never happens again. You decide to monitor your servers disk space. If the server
      has less than 15% of the disk space capacity, you want to be notified. Where can this be configured?

      A. Use Server Manager ➤ Alerts ➤ Alert when the physical disk space is under 15%.

      B. Use Server Manager ➤ Alerts ➤ Alert when the logical disk space is under 15%.

      C. Use Performance Monitor ➤ Alert View ➤ Alert when the physical disk space is
      under 15%.

      D. Use Performance Monitor ➤ Alert View ➤ Alert when the logical disk space is
      under 15%.

31   Your NT servers are all in a locked computer room. You are an administrator for the domain and
      are running the administrative tools on your Windows 95 computer. Which utility should you use
      to create shares on remote NT workstations?

      A. Explorer

      B. Server Manager

      C. User Manager for Domains

      D. File and Share Manager

32   You have configured your NT server with RAS. You will support a variety of Microsoft and non-Microsoft clients. You want each client to use the highest level of encryption as possible. Which option should you use when configuring encryption on the RAS server?

    A. Allow clients to specify encryption level.

    B. Allow any authentication including clear text.

    C. Require encrypted authentication.

    D. Require Microsoft encrypted authentication.

33   You have a mixture of clients that dial in to your RAS server. The clients are Microsoft and non-Microsoft clients. The non-Microsoft clients are able to send their RAS passwords through the CHAP authentication protocol. Based on this scenario, what is the highest level of security that could be imposed at the RAS server?

    A. Allow clients to specify encryption level.

    B. Allow any authentication including clear text.

    C. Require encrypted authentication.

    D. Require Microsoft encrypted authentication.

34   You are running SQL on your NT server. You have decided to optimize the server by configuring the Server optimization to Maximize Throughput For Network Applications. Where do you configure this option?

    A. Control Panel ➤ Network ➤ Services ➤ Server ➤ Properties

    B. Control Panel ➤ Services ➤ Server ➤ Properties

    C. Server Manager ➤ choose server ➤ Services ➤ Server ➤ Properties

    D. Control Panel ➤ Server

35 You have 20 users who need to access an accounting application that resides on a member server called ACCT. Your PDC is called ACME_PDC. Which steps should be completed to give your users access? Choose all that apply.

    A. On ACME_PDC create a global group called ACCOUNTING.

    B. On ACME_PDC create a local group called ACCOUNTING.

    C. On APPS create a global group called ACCT APP USERS.

    D. On APPS create a local group called ACCT APP USERS.

    E. Add the global group ACCOUNTING to the local group ACCT APP USERS.

    F. Add the local group ACCOUNTING to the global group ACCT APP USERS.

36 You are installing NT onto a new computer. The computer currently has no operating system installed. There is a SCSI CD-ROM drive that is attached to the computer. How should you proceed?

    A. Use the three setup floppies, then run `WINNT`.

    B. Boot from an NT boot diskette, then run `WINNT`.

    C. Use the three setup floppies, then run `WINNT32`.

    D. Boot from an NT boot diskette, then run `WINNT32`.

37 Your NT server uses disk mirroring for fault tolerance on your system and boot partition. You are creating an NT boot floppy that can be used in the event that your primary drive in the mirrored set fails. Which file will have to be edited?

    A. `SYSTEM.INI`

    B. `PROTOCOLS.INI`

    C. `BOOT.INI`

    D. `CONFIG.INI`

38   Your NT server uses disk duplexing for fault tolerance on your system and boot partition. You are creating an NT boot floppy that can be used in the event that your primary drive in the mirrored set fails. You have configured the system as shown here:

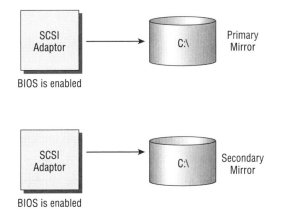

What will the ARC naming convention be for the secondary mirror?

   A. SCSI(1)DISK(1)RDISK(0)PARTITION(1)

   B. MULTI(1)DISK(1)RDISK(0)PARTITION(1)

   C. SCSI(1)DISK(0)RDISK(1)PARTITION(1)

   D. MULTI(1)DISK(0)RDISK(0)PARTITION(1)

39   Your network supports NT workstations and Windows 95 clients. Each client uses a Microsoft redirector. In addition, your network has several legacy NetWare servers. Which two pieces of software should be installed onto your NT server to allow your Microsoft clients access to the NetWare server?

   A. NWLink

   B. CSNW

   C. GSNW

   D. File and Print Services for NetWare

40 Your NT server is currently running version 3.51. When the server software was installed, it was installed to `C:\WINNT35`. What will happen if you upgrade to NT Server 4, and you specify the installation files should go to `C:\WINNT`?

   A. Make sure that you run `WINNT /U`, so that you can specify the previous directory and the new directory for the upgrade process.

   B. Make sure that you run `WINNT /R`, so that you can specify the previous directory and the new directory for the upgrade process.

   C. During the installation process, you can specify that you are upgrading, and NT will prompt you for the old directory and the new directory.

   D. You can't specify a different directory during an upgrade, if you go through with your plan, you'll end up with a dual-boot for your server between 3.51 and 4.0.

41 Your domain consists of a PDC and three BDCs. You store your logon scripts on the PDC, and want to ensure that users can access them, even if they authenticate to a BDC. What is the best solution?

   A. When you specify the logon script, use a UNC name that points to the PDC.

   B. Use the directory replicator service to copy the logon scripts to the BDCs.

   C. Use the `AT` command and schedule the logon scripts to be copied to the BDCs.

   D. Use the `WINAT` command and schedule the logon scripts to be copied to the BDCs.

42 You originally configured your NT workstations to be members of a workgroup. After using the workgroup model for a month, you decide that the decentralized administration is too much work. You now want to add them to the domain. Which two steps should you complete?

   A. Add the workstations to the domain through Server Manager.

   B. Add the workstations to the domain through Client Manager.

C. At the workstations, specify that the computer should be a part of the domain through Control Panel ➤ Network.

D. At the workstations, specify that the computer should be a part of the domain through Server Manager.

43 Your NT domain consists of a PDC, three BDCs and 100 Windows 95 clients. You are very concerned about security at the domain controllers and have specified in your policies book that only members of the Administrators group should be allowed to log on locally at the domain controllers. How can you technically enforce this?

A. Configure the Logon Workstations so that members of the Administrators group can only log on at the domain controllers.

B. In User Rights Policies on the PDC configure the Logon Locally right to only include the Administrators group.

C. Use Server Manger to specify that only members of the Administrators group can log on locally at the servers.

D. In User Rights Policies on the PDC configure the Access Domain Controller Locally right to only include the Administrators group.

44 You are concerned with fault tolerance so you are using disk striping with parity across five drives as your fault-tolerance solution. One of the drives fails. What should you do?

A. Replace the drive, then use Disk Administrator to regenerate the stripe set.

B. Use Disk Administrator to break the stripe set, replace the drive, then regenerate the stripe set.

C. Replace the drive, re-create the stripe set, then restore the data from tape backup.

D. Use Disk Administrator to break the stripe set, replace the drive, then restore the data from tape backup.

FINAL REVIEW

45   You have recently used Disk Administrator to create a new partition. As you are exiting the Disk Administrator utility, you receive a message stating that you should now update your emergency repair disk. What step do you take?

   A. Use the RDISK command to create a new emergency repair disk.

   B. Use the ERD command to create a new emergency repair disk.

   C. Use Disk Administrator ➤ Tools to create a new emergency repair disk.

   D. Use Server Manager ➤ Tools to create a new emergency repair disk.

46   Kaitlin is a member of the EVERYONE, SALES, and MANAGERS groups. The NTFS permissions on the C:\DATA directory allow the following access:

Everyone: No Access

Sales: Read

Managers: Change

Administrators: Full Control

What are Kaitlin's access rights to the C:\DATA folder?

   A. No Access

   B. Read

   C. Change

   D. Full Control

47 Your NT server contains a directory on C: called APPS. In this directory are subdirectories for SS, DB, WP, and EMAIL. You have just created a new share called APPS on the APPS directory. What is the default permissions that will be applied to EVERYONE?

A. No Access

B. Read

C. Change

D. Full Control

48 Recently, sensitive payroll information has been spreading among the employees. Several users have access to the payroll information, and you want to track anytime anyone of these users access this information and what type of access is used. The payroll information exists within an NTFS folder. You decide to implement NTFS auditing. What option must be set in User Manager for Domains first?

A. You must enable auditing for File and Object Access.

B. You must enable auditing for NTFS Object Access.

C. You must enable auditing for Use of User Rights.

D. You must enable auditing for NTFS Folder and File Access.

49 You are using Performance Monitor to track disk-related statistics. When you go to analyze the log, you realize all of the disk counters are flat. What step should you complete?

A. Use Disk Administrator ➤ Tools to enable disk counters.

B. Use the DISKPERF -y command to enable disk counters.

C. Use the DISKMON -y command to enable disk counters.

D. Use Server Manager ➤ Tools to enable disk counters.

50 Each of your departments has had a profile created that is shared by all users of the department. You specified that mandatory profiles be used since you didn't want one user to be able to edit the profile and affect the other users who share the same profile. The PDC that stores the profiles has crashed, so the users are logging in through BDCs. You have never implemented directory replication, so the profiles are only available on the PDC. What will happen to the users when they try to log on?

A. They will default back to their locally stored profiles.

B. They will receive a message stating that the mandatory profile is unavailable, and they will have the option of using their local profile.

C. The users will revert back to the default profile.

D. The users will not be able to log on.

51 Your network consists of a mixture of NT and NetWare servers. Your NetWare server is running an SQL server, which is a NetBIOS application. What software must be installed on your NT server to allow NT users to access this application?

A. NWLink IPX/SPX Compatible Transport

B. CSNW

C. GSNW

D. File and Print Services for NetWare

52 Your network consists of seven NetWare 3.12 servers. You are tired of the duplicate administration required with the client-server networking model. After evaluating several networking platforms, you have decided to update your network and use the NT domain model. The first step you take is to install an NT server as a PDC. You now wish to use the Migration Tool for NetWare to migrate your NetWare users and groups to your NT server. What must be installed on the NT server before you can use the migration tool? Choose all that apply.

A. You must be using the NWLink IPX/SPX compatible transport protocol.

B. You must have CSNW installed.

C. You must have GSNW installed.

D. You must have File and Print Services for NetWare installed.

53 You are using NT server as a print server. You have defined five printers on the print server. Your users are complaining because their jobs are not printing. You suspect a problem with the print spooler. What is the first action you should take to troubleshoot this problem?

A. Stop and restart the spooler service.

B. Delete the printers and re-create them; the printers may be corrupt.

C. Delete the print server, and re-create the print server.

D. Delete all jobs from the spooler, shut down and re-start the computer that is acting as the print server.

54 You network consists of a mixture of NetWare 3.11, NetWare 3.12, NetWare 4.1, NetWare 4.11, and NT 4.0 computers. The NetWare 3.11 servers use the Ethernet_802.3 frame types and the NetWare 3.12, NetWare 4.1, and NetWare 4.11 servers use the Ethernet_802.2 frame types. On your NT server, you are using NWLink IPX/SPX compatible transport protocol with the auto-detect frame type option. You are also using GSNW. Which of the NetWare servers will you be able to connect to? Choose all that apply.

A. The NetWare 3.11 servers

B. The NetWare 3.12 servers

C. The NetWare 4.1 servers

D. The NetWare 4.11 servers

55 Your NT server uses the NWLink IPX/SPX-compatible transport protocol and the TCP/IP protocol. You have decided to use Performance Monitor to watch your networking statistics. Your NT server is called NTSAPPS and you sit at an NT workstation called ADMIN. You want to do all monitoring from your workstation. What do you need to do to collect the networking statistics?

   A. Install the SNMP service on NTSAPPS.

   B. Install the SNMP service on ADMIN.

   C. Only specify the counters relating to NWLink and TCP/IP from Performance Monitor on NTSAPPS.

   D. Only specify the counters relating to NWLink and TCP/IP from Performance Monitor on ADMIN.

APPENDIX

Study Question and
Sample Test Answers

Unit 1 Answers

Study Questions

Planning Disk Drive Configurations

1. Duplexing

2. Mirroring

3. Disk mirroring (including duplexing)

4. Disk space: 2,000MB

   Parity information: 500MB

   Explanation: In disk striping with parity, you lose the sum of one drive. The space that is taken up is distributed among all of the drives in the stripe set, and used for storing parity information.

5. 1

6. 5

7. 2, 32

8. 3, 32

9. RAID 0: True

   RAID 1: True

   RAID 2: False

   RAID 3: False

   RAID 4: False

   RAID 5: True

10. Provides local security

    Supports compression

    Supports Macintosh volumes

    Supports NetWare migration

11. Backwards compatibility with operating systems like Windows 95 and DOS/Windows 3.*x*

12. RAID 0: FAT

    RAID 1: FAT and NTFS

    RAID 5: NTFS

Choosing Protocols

13. NWLink, TCP/IP

14. NetBEUI

15. DHCP

16. IP address

    subnet mask

    default gateway

17. Internal IPX address

    frame type

18. TCP/IP

19. NWLink

20. TCP/IP

Sample Test

1-1   D

Explanation: If you use disk striping (without fault tolerance) the required element will not be met since it is not fault tolerant.

1-2   A, B, C

Explanation: In order to access NetWare file and print resources, you must use CSNW or GSNW.

1-3   A

1-4   A, B, D

1-5   B

Explanation: With disk mirroring, the disk configuration will be fault tolerant and will support the system and boot partition. While you might see some performance gains on reads, you will see much slower performance on writes since you have one I\O channel that must write data to two drives.

1-6   B

Explanation: With disk striping with parity, you will have fault tolerance that also provides high performance. Disk striping with parity cannot be used on the system or boot partition.

1-7   B, C

1-8   B

1-9   C

1-10   C

1-11   C

Explanation: You will basically lose the sum of one drive that will be used to store parity information across the stripe set.

1-12   A

Explanation: Don't get fooled into thinking stripe set with parity. The question relates to a plain stripe set (with no parity) so the entire set is available for data.

1-13   C

Explanation: NTFS will support local security. It also supports Macintosh volumes and file compression. It cannot be used to dual-boot to Windows 95 since Windows 95 cannot read an NTFS partition.

1-14   D

Explanation: FAT can be used in a dual-boot environment with Windows 95. It does not support features such as local security, Macintosh support, or file compression when booted under NT.

1-15   A

Explanation: Since the question did not specify that fault tolerance was a requirement, disk striping will provide the maximum amount of data storage.

1-16   D

1-17   D

Explanation: Since you only have two drives, disk mirroring or disk duplexing are the only fault tolerant disk configurations you can use (disk striping with parity requires a minimum of three drives). Since you have two controllers, you would use disk duplexing.

1-18   A

Explanation: A stripe set only requires two drives. A stripe set with parity requires a minimum of three drives.

1-19   B

Explanation: A stripe set only requires two drives. A stripe set with parity requires a minimum of three drives.

1-20   C

Explanation: CONVERT is the only utility that will allow you to preserve data while changing the partition type to NTFS.

Unit 2 Answers

Study Questions

Installing an Intel-Based Server

1.   WINNT

   Explanation: WINNT is used since no previous OS was installed.

2.   WINNT32

   Explanation: WINNT32 is used since you are already running a 32-bit operating system.

3.   WINNT /b

4.   WINNT /ox

5.   True

   Explanation: Because you are already running NT, you can use the WINNT32 command. The only other key to the upgrade is that NT 4.0 should be installed to the same directory that NT 3.5 was installed in.

6.   False

   Explanation: There is no true upgrade path between Windows 95 and Windows NT. The Windows NT 4.0 Workstation Resource Guide contains a recommended migration path from Windows 95 to NT 4.0, but it is not an upgrade.

7.   Install the vendor's driver by using the Have Disk option.

8. \WINNT

9. FAT, NTFS

10. The emergency repair disk (ERD)

11. True

   Explanation: Windows NT Workstation can be upgraded to Windows NT Server.

12. Your system will not be upgraded, instead you will have created a multiboot configuration of NT Server 3.51 and NT Server 4.0.

NT Server Roles

13. PDC, BDCs

14. PDC

15. BDC

16. They are used to offload logon authentication, they provide fault tolerance

17. PDC, BDC, member server

18. The machine will not have the software administrative overhead of account management

19. False

   Explanation: Member servers cannot become domain controllers without a reinstallation of the Windows NT Server software.

20. False

   Explanation: The ideal situation during promotion is for the original PDC to be up and running, to allow the PDC role to be transfered, but it is not required.

21. False

Explanation: Because the BDC shares the same domain SID as the PDC, it cannot change domains.

22. True

Explanation: Since member servers do not contain the domain SID, they can change domains.

23. True

Explanation: Following the loss of the PDC, the BDCs hold an election, and if the BDC software versions are the same, the BDC that has been operating longest will win the election and will automatically become promoted.

24. Server Manager

25. One

Explanation: Each domain can contain one, and only one PDC. However, you can have as many BDCs as you want.

26. False

Explanation: BDCs are not required. It is recommended that you have at least one BDC for fault tolerance.

27. False

Explanation: Since the PDC and BDCs share the same domain SID, the PDC must be accessible to the BDC during installation.

28. True

Explanation: Member servers do not share the domain SID with the PDC. The PDC does not have to be accessible during a member servers installation.

Installation Methods for NT Server

29. False

Explanation: If you want to specify your paging files size and location, you must specify a custom installation.

30. Network Client Administrator

31. You must copy the installation files to a distribution point, you must create a network share from the distribution point.

32. False

Explanation: The network diskette contains a computer name that must be unique. If all 10 computers tried to use the same computer name, you'd have problems. However, you can use unattended answer and uniqueness difference files to automate the installation as these will differentiate items such as computer names.

33. Network Client for MS-DOS (includes Win 3.*x*), Windows for Workgroups, Windows 95, NT Workstation, NT Server

34. I386

Explanation: The I386 subdirectory contains the installation files for the Intel platform. Other subdirectories provide files for platforms such as Alpha and PowerPC.

35. False

Explanation: Intel platforms can be installed through CD-ROM or over-the-network.

36. False

Explanation: The Express installation will only recognize one network adapter card. To configure more than one adapter during installation, you must use the Custom installation option. You can, however, install NT Server configuring only one of the four network adapter cards initially, then configure the remaining three using the Hardware and Network Control Panels later.

37. False

Explanation: Domain controllers can be configured through the Express or Custom installation options.

Configuring Protocols and Protocol Bindings

38. TCP/IP

Explanation: TCP/IP requires you to configure the IP address, subnet mask, (and default gateway if needed). This could be simplified by using a DHCP server.

39. NetBEUI

Explanation: While NetBEUI requires no configuration, it also provides no support for routing, which makes this an unusable choice for a multiple segment network.

40. Incorrect frame type

Explanation: Besides the internal network number, which is not commonly used, the frame type is really the only thing you can mis-configure. If more than one frame type is being used, then the autodetect frame setting will only capture the first frame type that it sees, ignoring the others.

41. Ethernet_802.2

Explanation: NT tries to use Ethernet_802.2 since it is considered the industry standard. Netware servers running version 3.12 or later use a default frame type of 802.2. Earlier versions defaulted to 802.3.

42. Used to specify the gateway that should be used for routing TCP/IP packets outside of the originating subnet.

43. To automatically configure TCP/IP clients with at least an IP address.

44. Dynamic Host Configuration Protocol

45. IPCONFIG

46. IP address, subnet mask, default gateway

47. If you are using Microsoft Services (formerly File and Print Services) for NetWare or if you are using IPX routing.

48. NWLink internal network number, Ethernet frame type

49. Binding

50. By placing the most commonly used protocol at the top of the binding order they are selected first, thereby allowing you improved network performance.

51. The subnet mask is used to indicate which portion of the address should be used for the network address and which portion of the address identifies the unique host.

52. False

   Explanation: Selecting auto-frame detection when multiple frame types are being used in the NWLink protocol will result in the only the first frame type being detected and used.

53. Ethernet_802.2, Ethernet_802.3, Ethernet_II, Ethernet_SNAP

Configuring Network Adapters

54. Control Panel ➤ Network

55. IRQ, base I/O address, base memory address, DMA

56. Your network adapter will not be accessible

57. Router

58. False

   Explanation: Each adapter must have a unique IP addess.

Configuring NT Server Core Services

59. Only NT Server can act as an export computer

60. NT Server or NT Workstation

61. Backup Operator, Replicator

62. The export and the import computer must both run the replicator service

63. License Manager

64. NT Backup

65. True

Explanation: As long as the drive is shared and the server with the backup unit can access the share, network backups are possible.

66. True

67. Control Panel ➤ Services, Server Manager

68. NETLOGON

69. \WINNT\SYSTEM32\REPL\EXPORT

70. \WINNT\SYSTEM32\REPL\IMPORT

71. Per server, Per seat

72. Directory replication

73. Control Panel ➤ Network ➤ Services ➤ Server ➤ Properties

74. Balance

75. Maximize throughput for network applications

Configuring Peripherals and Devices

76. Control Panel

77. Network

78. Install and configure the driver for the SCSI adapter, install and configure the driver for the tape device

79. Uninterruptible Power SupplyUPS

Configuring Hard Disks

80. Disk striping

    Explanation: While disk striping will provide the most storage, it will provide no fault tolerance.

81. Disk striping with parity

82. Mirroring uses one controller and two drives, while duplexing provides further redundancy by using two controllers and two drives.

83. 1,200MB

    Explanation: In a volume set, the partitions do not have to be the same size, so you can utilize all the space that is available.

84. multi (0)

85. multi (0)

86. scsi (0)

87. False

    Explanation: The CONVERT utility is a one-way process, from FAT to NTFS

88. 900MB

    Explanation: In a stripe set, all partitions must be the same size, so you must take the smallest size, 300MB. Since no parity is being used, you can use all 900MB for data storage.

89. BOOT.INI

90. multi(0)disk(0)rdisk(1)partition(2)

Explanation: Because you are using IDE you use Multi, this automatically makes Disk 0. The first drive is 0, the second drive is 1 so Rdisk is 1. Within the disk, partitions are labeled 1 and 2. Because the boot partition is on E:\, it is labeled the Partition 2.

91. multi(0)disk(0)rdisk(0)partition(1)

Explanation: Because the BIOS is enabled on the SCSI adapter you use Multi, because you are using Multi, Disk is automatically 0, because it is the first disk, Rdisk is 0 and the first partition is always numbered 1.

92. scsi(0)disk(0)rdisk(0)partition(2)

Explanation: Because the BIOS is disabled on the SCSI adapter you use SCSI. On the first controller Disk will be 0. Because you are using SCSI, Rdisk is automatically 0. The boot partition is on the second partition within the drive, so it is 0.

93. 600MB

Explanation: The stripe set itself is 900MB, however the parity information will take up the sum of one drive, or 300MB. This leaves 600MB available for data storage.

94. CONVERT

95. Volume set

Configuring Printers

96. False, False, True, True, True, True

97. The printers should be in close proximity and they are all required to use the same print driver.

98. Network Print Server

Explanation: My Computer is used to create a new network printer. The Network Print Server option is used to connect to an existing network printer.

99. Ports

100. Scheduling

101. General

102. Setup two printers, allow the Managers group to use one printer, which has a higher priority. Allow the Sales group to use the other printer which has a lower priority.

103. My Computer is used to create a new local printer which can then be share as a network printer. The Network Print Server option is used to connect to an existing network printer.

Configuring NT Server for Various Clients

104. True

105. False

Explanation: Only NT computers have computer accounts in an NT domain.

106. Server Manager

107. Control Panel ➢ Network ➢ Identification tab

108. Network Client Administrator

109. False

Sample Test

2-1   A

2-2   B

2-3   A

Explanation: Each partition in the stripe set must be the same logical size. This means that you will use three 500 MB partitions. You will lose the sum of one drive for parity, which means 1,000 MB is available for data storage.

2-4 C

Explanation: Each partition in the stripe set must be the same logical size. This means that you will use three 500 MB partitions. Since you are not using parity, the entire stripe set can be used to store data.

2-5 D

Explanation: In a volumes set, the partition sizes do not have to match, so all available space can be used.

2-6 B

Explanation: In the stripe set, all partitions must be the same size. This question asks how much space the parity will take up, which is the sum of one drive (partition) which is 500MB.

2-7 A

2-8 B

2-9 B

2-10 B

2-11 D

Explanation: CONVERT is the only utility that allows you to preserve existing data while changing a FAT partition to NTFS.

2-12 B

Explanation: WINNT32 is used whenever you are already running NT as your operating system. The \ox switch is used to create the startup floppies without running through the entire NT installation routine.

2-13 D

2-14 C

2-15 C

Explanation: You can't specify a UNC path for logon scripts. You must use directory replication to copy the logon scripts from one location (usually the PDC) to other domain controllers.

2-16   D

2-17   A,C

2-18   D

2-19   B

2-20   A

2-21   B

Explanation: In order to upgrade NT, it must be installed into the same directory as the previous version of NT. If you install it to a new directory, you will end up with a dual-boot configuration.

2-22   B,C

2-23   C,D,E

2-24   C

2-25   B,C

2-26   D

Explanation: Since auto-detect will only select a single frame type, you must manually configure NWLink IPX/SPX and choose the two frame types you will need to support.

2-27   D

Explanation: In order to change a domain controller to a member server, the only option you have is to re-install the computer.

2-28   A,D

2-29   A,B,C,D

2-30   B

2-31   A

Unit 3 Answers

Study Questions

User and Group Management

1. User Manager for Domains

2. Disable the account in User Manager for Domains

3. %USERNAME%

4. False

   Explanation: NT user rights define the system tasks that a user can perform. To specify access rights to NTFS folders and files, you would use local NTFS permissions.

5. Backup files and directories

   Restore files and directories

6. Allows a user to logon at the local computer

7. Administrators

8. Policies ➤ User Rights

9. Global

10. Global groups can only contain users from within its domain database.

11. To prevent unauthorized users from trying to break into your system.

12. Within password restrictions, you would set password uniqueness

13. Event Viewer, Security log

14. Local

15. Administrator

Guest

16. Password never expires

17. Users from the local SAM database, users from within the domain, users from trusted domains, global groups from within the domain, and global groups from trusted domains

18. NETLOGON

19. Administrators

20. Specify that only the Administrators group has the "shut down the system" user right

21. Administrators and Server Operators

22. On NT domain controllers

23. On any NT computer

24. Local

Global

Global, local

25. 14

26. The administrator must unlock the account

27. Security

28. Administrators

29. Configure the Log On To user property and specify the NetBIOS computer names at which the user could log on

30. User and group management

31. Administrators and Account Operators

32. Log off and log on again

Policies and Profiles

33. `\WINNT\PROFILES\%USERNAME%`

34. Local

35. `\WINNT\SYSTEM32\REPL\IMPORT\SCRIPTS`

36. Rename the `NTUSER.DAT` file to `NTUSER.MAN`

37. Registry

38. Users

Groups

Computers

39. `NTUSER.DAT`

40. `NTCONFIG.POL`

41. User Manager for Domains

Explanation: In User Manager for Domains, you specify the user who will use the roaming profile, and in the Profile dialog box, use a UNC name to point to the roaming profile location.

42. System Policy Editor

Remote Administration

43. User Manager for Domains

Server Manager

Event Viewer

44. NT Explorer

My Computer

45. Server Manager

46. Server Manager

47. True

48. False

Explanation: Disk Administrator cannot be used for remote administration.

49. Windows 95 clients

Windows NT Workstations

Disk Resource Management

50. No Access

Read

Change

Full Control

51. False

Explanation: Share permissions can only be applied to folders.

52. Change

Explanation: In this case, Rick would have the combination of rights and Change includes Read.

53. No Access

Explanation: If a user has No Access through user or group memberships, then it doesn't matter what their other permissions are, they will have No Access.

54. The file will receive the permissions from the destination directory

Explanation: Technically a move from one partition to another is a copy, then the original file is deleted, so the move is actually a copy.

55. The file will inherit the permissions of the source directory

56. The file will receive the permissions from the destination directory

57. The file will receive the permissions from the destination directory

58. True

59. False

Explanation: You can only audit files on NTFS partitions.

60. Event Viewer, Security log

61. Change

62. Group Everyone has Full Control

63. Group Everyone has Full Control

64. Special Directory Access

65. File and object access

66. False

Explanation: Permissions are only applied to files within the folder by default.

67. True

68. True

69. Administrators

Server Operators

Sample Test

3-1   B

Explanation: You can only limit logon hours on a per-user basis.

3-2   C, D

3-3   A

3-4   B

3-5   A

3-6   D

3-7   D

Explanation: The UNC path is always *computername**sharename*, and would not include the domain name. The variable for user name is %username%.

3-8   C, E

3-9   D

3-10   A

3-11   A, D

Explanation: Power Users is only available on NT workstations.

3-12   B

3-13   B, D, F

3-14   A, C, E

3-15   A

3-16   A

3-17	D
3-18	A
3-19	A
3-20	A
3-21	B
3-22	B, D
3-23	B
3-24	D
3-25	C

Unit 4 Answers

Study Questions

NetWare Connectivity

1. GSNW

2. NTGATEWAY

   Explanation: In addition, you must create a user on the NetWare server that will be used to specify the gateway. This user must belong to the NTGATEWAY group on the Net-Ware server.

3. You must be using the NWLink IPX/SPX compatible transport protocol

4. One

   Explanation: Regardless of the number of users who connect through the gateway, only one NetWare connection or license is used.

5. False

   Explanation: Its the other way around, the NetWare objects are migrated to an NT server.

6. False

7. True

8. True

9. False

10. False

11. True

12. You must specify an NTFS destination directory.

    Explanation: NTFS is required since FAT does not support local permissions.

13. Create and use a mapping file.

14. False

    Explanation: NetWare users and groups must be migrated to an NT server that is a domain controller.

15. NWLink IPX/SPX Compatible Transport, GSNW

16. False

    Explanation: In order for NetWare users to access NT resources, you have to use the File and Print Services for NetWare product.

17. NWLink IPX/SPX Compatible Transport

18. NWLink IPX/SPX Compatible Transport, File and Print Services for NetWare

19. Use the Trial Migration option

    Explanation: A trial migration will complete all of the steps for the actual migration except the write at the end. This allows you to see any errors that would occur during the migration so that you can correct the errors before any commitments are made.

20. Overwrite with new info

21. Ignore

22. GSNW

23. True

24. True

25. True

26. False

27. False

28. True

29. Administrators

30. Through Control Panel ➤ Network ➤ Services ➤ Add service

31. You should specify the user account that was created on the NetWare server and belongs to the NTGATEWAY group.

32. Add Supervisors to the Administrators group.

33. Use Supervisor Defaults

34. Pop-up errors

    Verbose User/Group logging

    Verbose File logging

Remote Access Server

35. PSTN

    ISDN

    Serial null modem cables

    X.25

    PPTP

36. Remote Access Admin

    User Manager for Domains

37. Preset to:

38. Require Microsoft encrypted authentication

39. PPP

    Explanation: SLIP is not installed on the RAS server since the RAS server cannot accept clients dialing in with SLIP, only PPP.

40. SLIP

41. NetBEUI

42. Use the Set By Caller option

43. TCP/IP

    Explanation: TCP/IP supports applications using the Win Socks API. In addition, it should be bound first if you are using multiple protocols.

44. Nothing, only the IP address

45. True

    True

    False

46. False

47. MS-CHAP

48. Require Microsoft encrypted authentication

Explanation: This is the only authentication and encryption method that supports data encryption.

49. True

Explanation: A client configured with the Accept any authentication method including clear text can supply the authenticating server with any authentication and encryption that is requested.

50. NetBEUI

IPX

TCP/IP

Sample Test

4-1   C

4-2   B

Explanation: Choices C and D are not valid choices on a RAS server. B is correct since it is the only authentication and encryption method that supports data encryption.

4-3   D

Explanation: Through the NWLink protocol, you can access NetBIOS applications, but you have no file and print access.

4-4   B

4-5   A

4-6   A

Explanation: Since you don't know what client platforms are dialing in, you should select A. The key is that access was more important than security.

4-7   B, C

4-8   A

Explanation: If you want to specify more advance IP configuration, you should install a DHCP server and specify that the clients get their information from the DHCP server.

4-9   C

4-10   C

4-11   D

4-12   A

Explanation: SLIP is not accepted as a dial-in protocol and TCP/IP and IPX/SPX are not WAN protocols.

4-13   B

4-14   B

Explanation: SLIP doesn't have all of the features of PPP, but it is commonly used with UNIX servers and it provides the lowest overhead.

4-15   D

Explanation: The choice for A, B, and C do not exist, which leaves D as the best and only option.

4-16   A, C, D

4-17   A, B, E, F

4-18   A

4-19 C

Explanation: D is invalid because only members of the Administrators group can perform a NetWare migration.

4-20 A, B, C

Unit 5 Answers

Study Questions

Monitoring and Optimization

1. SNMP

    Explanation: You must install the SNMP service on the computer that the TCP/IP statistics are being reported on.

2. Log view

3. Not enough RAM

4. Run DISKPERF -y

    Restart the computer

5. 80%

6. Processor

    Memory

    Disk

    Network

7. Chart

8. Upgrade your processor

   Add another processor

9. Cache object, Data Map Hits

   Memory object, Pages/Sec

   Explanation: There are more possible answers to this question. These were the two options that were featured in the overview. For other possible answers, refer to the Performance Monitor help documentation.

10. Use the Alert View of Performance Monitor to receive notification.

11. Use disk striping without parity

    Use faster disks and controllers

    Balance your disk I/O requirements (file storage) over multiple channels

12. Chart

    Alert

    Log

    Report

Sample Test

5-1 D

   Explanation: If %Processor Time is at 15%, then there is no bottleneck indicated. You would only be concerned if this number were 80% or higher.

5-2 C

5-3 A, D

   Explanation: In order to collect TCP/IP statistics, you must install the SNMP service on the computer you are collecting the statistics on.

5-4 A

5-5   A

5-6   D

5-7   D

Explanation: Whenever you have a memory-related problem (in this case, excessive caching), you should always add RAM as the best solution.

5-8   C, D

5-9   A, B

5-10   D

Unit 6 Answers

Study Questions

Troubleshooting Installation Errors

1. False

    Explanation: NT is an i/o intensive operating system and minor problems in other operating systems can become magnified under NT. The best suggestion is to verify that all of your hardware is on the HCL.

2. Hardware Compatibility List (HCL)

3. False

    Explanation: Since the PDC has the only read-write copy of the SAM database, computer accounts can only be added to the SAM PDC.

4. During installation, do not have NT detect your mass storage device. Specify that you will identify the storage device, then provide the NT driver that was supplied by the SCSI adapter manufacturer.

5. base i/o address

   base memory address

   DMA

6. `BOOT.INI`

   `NTOSKRNL.EXE`

7. `NTLDR`

8. Use the NT Boot floppies to access the Repair option, then use the ERD to verify and restore the missing files.

9. `BOOT.INI`

10. `BOOTSECT.DOS`

11. `NTDETECT.COM`

12. `NTLDR`

13. `BOOTSECT.DOS`

14. `NTBOOTDD.SYS`

Troubleshooting Configuration Errors

15. The Event Viewer

16. Windows NT Diagnostics

17. Application log

18. During the boot process, hit the space bar when prompted.

19. `RDISK`

20. False

    Explanation: In order to use the ERD, you must boot to the NT Boot diskettes and choose the R option for repair.

21. System

    Security

    Application

22. False

    Explanation: The top errors are the latest errors. If multiple errors occur, check the oldest error first since it may be a dependency for the other errors.

23. Server Manager

24. Control Panel ➤ Network ➤ Protocols tab

25. True

    Explanation: The ERD is unique to each computer and contains portions of each computer's unique registry.

26. Windows NT Diagnostics

27. Server Manager

    Explanation: If you guessed Control Panel ➤ Services of the Windows NT Diagnostics ➤ Services tab, you are wrong because these utilities cannot be used to manage the services on remote computers, as they only work on local computers.

Troubleshooting Printer Errors

28. You had installed the incorrect print driver.

29. Stop and restart the spooler service.

30. From the Print Server properties, access the Advanced tab, and specify an alternate folder for the spool file.

31. Create a new port on the print server and specify the UNC port of the failed printer.

Troubleshooting RAS Errors

32. PPP

    Explanation: RAS clients can use SLIP or PPP to dial-in to remote servers, but NT RAS will only accept incoming PPP connections.

33. Allow any authentication including clear text.

34. You must enable the log through the Registry.

35. \winnt\system23\ras

36. Remote Access Admin

    User Manager for Domains

37. Remote Access Admin

Troubleshooting Connectivity Problems

38. Incorrect frame type

39. Ethernet_802.2

    Ethernet_802.3

    Ethernet_II

    Ethernet_SNAP

40. IP address

    subnet mask

    default gateway

41. PING

42. TRACERT

43. IPCONFIG

Troubleshooting Resource Access and Permissions Problems

44. NTFS permissions

Explanation: Share permissions will not be applied if you access the resource locally.

45. Whichever set of permissions is more restrictive.

46. No Access

Explanation: If you have the No Access permission assigned to your user account or any groups you belong to, then it doesn't matter if you have other access permissions, No Access will prevent access of the resource.

47. Kevin needs to logout and logon again to update his access token.

48. When permissions were applied, the Replace Permissions on Subdirectories was not checked, so the default permissions that Everyone has Full Control are still assigned.

Resolving Disk Failures in a Fault-Tolerant Environment

49. Failure of the primary partition

Explanation: Failure of the secondary partition is less labor intensive because the BOOT.INI and ARC name are still valid.

50. Replace the failed drive, use Disk Administrator to regenerate the stripe set using the free space on the new drive.

51. At this point, you would have to replace the hardware, establish a new stripe set with parity, and restore your data from tape backup.

52. Break the mirror set through Disk Administrator and delete the failed partition, replace the failed hard drive, use the Disk Administrator to establish a new mirror with the free space on the new drive.

53. Boot with the NT boot diskette you created prior to the failure, use Disk Administrator to break the mirror set and delete the failed partition, copy the BOOT.INI from the floppy disk to the system partition, replace the failed hardware, and finally using the free space on the new drive, establish a new mirror set.

54. The NT Backup program

55. BOOT.INI

Sample Test

6-1   D

Explanation: If you have used Disk Administrator and your system fails to boot, suspect the BOOT.INI file first. By adding logical partitions, you can cause the ARC name to change. When using Disk Administrator, pay careful attention to the exit messages, because you will be warned if the BOOT.INI needs to be edited, and if so, what the edits should be. Many times users ignore this message.

6-2   A

6-3   C

6-4   D

6-5   C

6-6   C

6-7   D

Explanation: If the gateway were configured improperly, you would still see the NetWare server, you would just receive an error when you tried to access the resources.

6-8   C

6-9   C

Explanation: Through the NTFS permissions she can Change since she is part of Accounting Managers. Through the share permissions she has, Full Control Access permissions will be the more restrictive of the access permissions.

6-10   A

Explanation: Because Wendy is a part of the Accounting Temps group, and they have been assigned No Access, Wendy is governed by the No Access permission.

6-11   B

Explanation: If two drives fail, then your only option is to recreate the stripe set and restore the data from tape backup.

6-12   B

Explanation: WINNT32 can only be run from within NT. The /ox option specifies that you want to create the three floppies without actually going through the entire installation process.

6-13   C

6-14   A

Explanation: If the secondary drive fails, you use the same steps you would use to recover from a data-only mirror since the BOOT.INI file does not need to be edited.

6-15   D

6-16   D

Explanation: By default, the oldest events will be at the bottom of the list and the newest events will be recorded at the top of the list. You should try and identify the first error since it may be a dependency for other errors that are occuring.

6-17   A

6-18   B

6-19   A

6-20   B

6-21   D

6-22   A

6-23   D

6-24   B

Unit 7 Answers

Sample Test

1.   A

Explanation: The spool file is a property of the Print Server. To specify the print server spool file, you open the printers window and select Server Properties, then choose the Advanced tab. You could edit this through the Registry Editor as well, but the rule is you should edit through GUI utilities if possible, and only use the Registry Editor if no other alternative exists.

2.   C

Explanation: By defining a separator page, the printer is able to switch modes properly.

3.   C

Explanation: The ERD can be used to repair the NT boot files, but it is not a bootable disk, and requires the three setup files. To make the three setup files you can access the NT CD and type WINNT /ox. To update your emergency repair disk, you type RDISK from a command prompt on the computer that the ERD is being made for.

4.   B

5. C

Explanation: There are no GUI utilities that allow you to convert a FAT partition to NTFS. This makes C the only option. If you were to use the FORMAT command, you'd lose all of your data.

6. C

7. B

8. C

9. A

Explanation: By default the emergency repair disk only contains portions of the registry. You can backup the registry through the Registry Editor, but not through the method specified. You shouldn't backup the registry through the Registry Editor anyway since the registry would be open and the backup would not be reliable. The NT Backup utility is proven to reliably backup the registry.

10. C

Explanation: The backup is caused by the amount of data being sent to one computer. By dividing the load and adding a second backup unit to a second machine, backups will be completed in a more timely manner.

11. D

Explanation: Disk mirroring and disk duplexing have 100% overhead in storage requirements. Disk striping provides no fault tolerance. Disk striping with parity has lower disk overhead in terms of fault tolerance while also boosting performance due to the striping of data.

12. A

Explanation: Don't confuse striping with striping with parity. Striping requires two drives. Striping with parity requires three drives. The only time you require multiple controllers is with disk duplexing.

13. C

14. B

15. D

16. D

Explanation: Anytime you have excessive paging, adding memory is the best solution. Paging is due to lack of memory. Choice A, B, and C might help to a limited degree, but its similar to treating the symptoms rather than the problem.

17. C

18. A, D

Explanation: The long file name will be copied since NT supports long file names, but the permissions will be lost since FAT does not support local permissions.

19. B, D

Explanation: The key to this question is that you are moving to another NTFS partition. In this case, the move is actually a copy and permissions and attributes are handled as copies, meaning the destination directories permissions and attributes will be applied.

20. A, C

Explanation: The key to this question is that the source and destination directory are on the same NTFS partition.

21. A

22. B, C

Explanation: The system and boot partition cannot be a part of a stripe set, so even though option D provides fault tolerance, it cannot be used.

23. B

Explanation: The chart and report view are used to monitor events in real-time.

24. A, D

25. D

Explanation: This confuses many people since it appears as if you can specify profile type in Control Panel ➤ System ➤ Profiles tab, but this is mainly used to copy profiles from one location to another.

26. D

27. D

Explanation: Once a member server, always a member server, unless you re-install.

28. B

Explanation: Since you only define one logical printer for the pool, you can only define one print driver. As long as all of the printers can use that driver, they don't necessarily have to be the same make and model.

29. C

30. D

31. B

Explanation: The only utility that is used to create remote shares in NT 4.0 is Server Manager. If you are using the NT Administrative Tools, you can use Explorer to modify NTFS permissions or to manage network printers.

32. B

Explanation: The key is that you are supporting non-Microsoft clients. In this case, you have to allow any encryption, including clear text.

33. C

34. A

35. A, D, E

Explanation: The NT way of managing groups:

Create a local group on the computer that contains the resource, assign permissions.

Create a global group on the PDC for the domain, add users.

Add the global group to the local group.

36. A

Explanation: The three setup floppies contain the NT drivers for installation media (CDs), so by using the three setup floppies, you can access the CD to complete the NT installation.

37. C

Explanation: You will need to edit BOOT.INI so you can point to the ARC path of the second drive in the mirrored set.

38. D

39. A, C

40. D

41. B

Explanation: You can't specify a UNC name for logon scripts, you must use the Directory Replicator.

42. A, C

43. B

44. A

45. A

46. A

Explanation: If your user account or any groups you belong to have been assigned the No Access right, then you will have No Access, regardless or other permissions you might have been assigned.

47. D

48. A

49. B

50. D

51. A

Explanation: Through NWLink alone, you can access NetBIOS applications.

52. A, C

53. A

Explanation: This usually fixes the problem, and in troubleshooting, you want to try simple solutions first.

54. B, C, D

Explanation: Auto-detect will only select one frame type. In this example, the type is Ethernet_802.2. Since this is the case, the NT users will not see servers using the Ethernet_802.3 frame type. To see all servers, you should use manual configuration and select both frame types.

55. A

Explanation: To enable TCP/IP counters, you must install the SNMP service on the computer where you will be collecting the statistics.

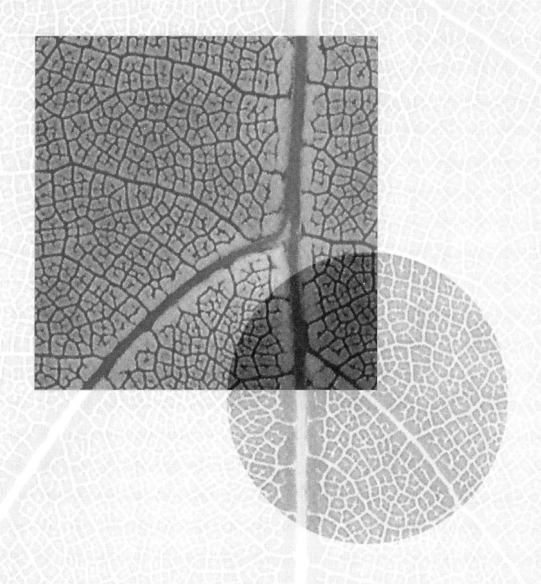

Glossary

Access Control Entries (ACE)   Each Access Control List (ACL) has an associated ACE which lists the permissions that have been granted or denied to the users and groups listed in the ACL. See *Access Control List*.

Access Control List (ACL)   Lists of security identifiers contained by objects that allow only certain processes—those identified in the list as having the appropriate permission—to activate the services of that object. See *Object, Security Identifier, Permissions*.

Access Tokens   Objects containing the security identifier of a running process. A process started by another process inherits the starting process's access token. The access token is checked against each object's ACL to determine whether or not appropriate permissions are granted to perform any requested service. See *Access Control List, Access Control Entries, permissions, object, Security Identifier, Process*.

Account Lockout   Used to specify how many invalid logon attempts should be tolerated before a user account is locked out. Account lockout is set through User Manager for Domains. See *Security, User Manager for Domains*.

Account Policies   Account policies are used to determine password and logon requirements. Account policies are set through User Manager for Domains. See *User Manager for Domains*.

Accounts   Containers for security identifiers, passwords, permissions, group associations, and preferences for each user of a system. The User Manager for Domains utility is used to administer accounts. See *Security Identifier, Preferences, Permissions, Passwords, Groups*.

ACE   See *Access Control Entries*.

ACL   See *Access Control List*.

Adapter   Any hardware device that allows communications to occur through physically dissimilar systems. This term usually refers to peripheral cards that are permanently mounted inside computers and provide an interface from the computer's bus to another media such as a hard disk or a network. See *Network Interface Card, SCSI*.

Address Resolution Protocol (ARP)   An Internet protocol for resolving an IP address into a Physical layer address (such as an Ethernet media access controller address). See *Physical layer, Internet Protocol.*

Administrative Tools   A program group on NT domain controllers that contains utilities such as User Manager for Domains, Server Manager, Disk Administrator, Performance Monitor, and Network Monitor. See *User Manager for Domains, Server Manager, Disk Administrator, Performance Monitor, Network Monitor.*

ADMINISTRATOR Account   A special account in Windows NT that has the ultimate set of security permissions and can assign any permission to any user or group. The ADMINISTRATOR account is used to correct security problems. See *Permissions.*

Administrators   Users who are part of the ADMINISTRATORS group. This group has the ultimate set of security permissions. See *Administrator Account, Permissions, Groups.*

Advanced Research Projects Agency Network (ARPANET)   Predecessor to the Internet that was developed by the Department of Defense in the late 1960's.

AppleTalk   The built-in (to firmware) suite of network protocols used by Macintosh computers. Windows NT Server uses AppleTalk to service Macintosh clients by simulating an Apple server. See *Macintosh, Network Protocol.*

Applications   Large software packages that perform a specific function, such as word processing, Web browsing, or database management. Applications typically consist of more than one program. See *Programs.*

Application Layer   The layer of the OSI model that interfaces with User mode programs called applications by providing high-level network services based upon lower-level network layers. Network file systems like named pipes are an example of Application-layer software. See *Named Pipes, OSI Model, Application.*

ARP   See *Address Resolution Protocol.*

ARPANET   See *Advanced Research Projects Agency Network.*

Asymmetrical Multiprocessing   A multiple processor architecture in which certain processors are designated to run certain threads or in which scheduling is not done on a fair-share basis. Asymmetrical multiprocessing is easier to implement than symmetrical multiprocessing, but does not scale well as processors are added. See *Microprocessor, Symmetrical Multiprocessing.*

Asynchronous Transfer Mode (ATM)   A wide area transport protocol that runs at many different speeds and supports real-time, guaranteed packet delivery in hardware, as well as lower-quality levels of service on a bandwidth-available basis. ATM will eventually replace all other wide area protocols, as most worldwide PTSN providers have declared their support for the international standard. See *Public Switched Telephone Network, Wide Area Network.*

ATM   See *Asynchronous Transfer Mode.*

Audit Policy   Audit policy determines which user events you wish to track for security reasons. Audit policy can track the success or failure of specified security events; it is set in the User Manager for Domains. See *Security, User Manager for Domains.*

Backup   The process of writing all the data contained in online mass storage devices to offline mass storage devices for the purpose of safe keeping. Backups are usually performed from hard disk drives to tape drives. Also referred to as archiving. See *Hard Disk Drive.*

Backup Browser   A computer on a Microsoft network that maintains a list of computers and services available on the network. The Master Browser supplies this list. The backup browser distributes the Browsing service load to a workgroup or domain. See *Master Browser.*

Backup Domain Controllers   Servers that contain accurate replications of the security and user databases; these servers can authenticate workstations in the absence of a primary domain controller (PDC). See *Primary Domain Controller.*

Baseline   A snapshot record of your computer's current performance statistics that can be used for analysis and planning purposes.

Basic Input/Output System (BIOS)   A set of routines in firmware that provides the most basic software interface drivers for hardware attached to the computer. The BIOS contains the bootstrap routine. See *Boot, Driver, Firmware.*

Bindery   A NetWare structure that contains user accounts and permissions. It is similar to the Security Accounts Manager in Windows NT. See *Security Accounts Manager*.

Binding   The process of linking network services to network service providers. The binding facility allows users to define exactly how network services operate in order to optimize the performance of the system. By default, Windows enables all possible bindings. The Network control panel is used to change bindings. See *Network Layer, Data Link Layer*.

BIOS   See *Basic Input/Output System*.

Bit   A binary digit. A numeral having only two possible values, 0 or 1. Computers represent these two values as high (voltage present) or low (no voltage present) state on a control line. Bits are accumulated in sets of certain sizes to represent higher values. See *Byte*.

Boot   The process of loading a computer's operating system. Booting usually occurs in multiple phases, each successively more complex until the entire operating system and all its services are running. Also called bootstrap. The computer's BIOS must contain the first level of booting. See *Basic Input/Output System*.

Boot Partition   The boot partition is the partition that contains the system files. The system files are located in **C:\WINNT** by default. See *Partition, System Partition*.

BOOTP   See *Bootstrap Protocol*.

Bootstrap Protocol (BOOTP)   Predecessor to the DHCP protocol. BOOTP was used to assign IP addresses to diskless workstations. See *Dynamic Host Configuration Protocol*.

Bottlenecks   Components operating at their peak capacity that restrict the flow of information through a system. Used singularly, the term indicates the single most restrictive component in a system.

Bridge   A device that connects two networks of the same Data Link protocol by forwarding those packets destined for computers on the other side of the bridge. See *Router, Data Link Layer*.

Browser A computer on a Microsoft network that maintains a list of computers and services available on the network.

Browsing The process of requesting the list of computers and services on a network from a browser.

Caching A speed optimization technique that keeps a copy of the most recently used data in a fast, high-cost, low-capacity storage device rather than in the device upon which the actual data resides. Caching assumes that recently used data is likely to be used again. Fetching data from the cache is faster than fetching data from the slower, larger storage device. Most caching algorithms also copy next-most-likely to be used data and perform write caching to further increase speed gains. See *Write-Back Caching, Write-Through Caching*.

CD-ROM See *Compact Disk-Read Only Memory*.

Central Processing Unit (CPU) The central processing unit of a computer. In microcomputers such as IBM PC compatible machines, the CPU is the microprocessor. See *Microprocessor*.

Client A computer on a network that subscribes to the services provided by a server. See *Server*.

Client Services for NetWare (CSNW) A service provided with Windows NT that connects an NT client to NetWare file servers. See *NetWare, Client Services for NetWare*.

Client/Server A network architecture that dedicates certain computers called servers to act as service providers to computers called clients, which users operate to perform work. Servers can be dedicated to providing one or more network services such as file storage, shared printing, communications, e-mail service, and Web response. See *Share, Peer*.

Client/Server Applications Applications that split large applications into two components: computer-intensive processes that run on application servers and user interfaces that run on clients. Client/server applications communicate over the network through interprocess communication mechanisms. See *Client, Server, Interprocess Communications*.

Code Synonymous with software but used when the software is the object of discussion, rather than the utility it provides. See *Software*.

COM Port   Communications port. A serial hardware interface conforming to the RS-232 standard for low-speed serial communications. See *Modem, Serial.*

Compact Disk-Read Only Memory (CD-ROM)   A media for storing extremely large software packages on optical read-only discs. CD-ROM is an adaptation of the CD medium used for distributing digitized music. CD-ROM discs can hold up to 650MB of information and cost very little to produce in mass quantity. See *Hard Disk Drive.*

Components   Interchangeable elements of a complex software or hardware system. See *Module.*

Compression   A space optimization scheme that reduces the size (length) of a data set by exploiting the fact that most useful data contains a great deal of redundancy. Compression reduces redundancy by creating symbols smaller than the data they represent and an index that defines the value of the symbols for each compressed set of data.

Computer   A device capable of performing automatic calculations based upon lists of instructions called programs. The computer feeds the results of these calculations (output) to peripheral devices that can represent them in useful ways, such as graphics on a screen or ink on paper. See *Microprocessor.*

Computer Name   A 1-15 character NetBIOS name used to uniquely identify a computer on the network. See *Network Basic Input/Output System.*

Control Panel   A software utility that controls the function of specific operating system services by allowing users to change default settings for the service to match their preferences. The Registry contains the Control Panel settings on a system and/or per-user basis. See *Registry, Account.*

Cooperative Multitasking   A multitasking scheme in which each process must voluntarily return time to a central scheduling route. If any single process fails to return to the central scheduler, the computer will lock up. Both Windows and the Macintosh operating system use this scheme. See *Preemptive Multitasking, Windows for Workgroups 3.11.*

CPU   See *Microprocessor.*

CSNW   See *Client Services for NetWare.*

Data Link Control (DLC)   An obsolete network transport protocol that allows PCs to connect to older IBM mainframes and HP printers. See *TCP/IP*.

Data Link Layer   In the OSI model, the layer that provides the digital interconnection of network devices and the software that directly operates these devices, such as network interface adapters. See *Physical Layer, Network Layer, OSI Model*.

Database   A related set of data organized by type and purpose. The term also can include the application software that manipulates the data. The Windows NT Registry (a database itself) contains a number of utility databases such as user account and security information. See *Registry*.

DDE   See *Dynamic Data Exchange*.

Default Shares   Resources shared by default when Windows NT is installed. See *Share, Resource*.

Desktop   A directory that the background of the Windows Explorer shell represents. By default the desktop contains objects that contain the local storage devices and available network shares. Also a key operating part of the Windows GUI. See *Explorer, Shell*.

DHCP   See *Dynamic Host Configuration Protocol*.

Dial-Up Connections   Data Link-layer digital connections made via modems over regular telephone lines. The term *dial-up* refers to temporary digital connections, as opposed to leased telephone lines, which provide permanent connections. See *Data Link Layer, Public Switched Telephone Network, Modem*.

Directories   In a file system directories are containers that store files or other directories. Mass storage devices have a root directory that contains all other directories, thus creating a hierarchy of directories sometimes referred to as a *directory tree*. See *File, File System*.

Directory Replication   The process of copying a directory structure from an import computer to an export computer(s). Anytime changes are made to the export computer, the import computer(s) is automatically updated with the changes.

Disk Administrator   Graphical utility used to manage disks.

Disk Duplexing   Disk duplexing is similar to disk mirroring, but in addition to the features of disk mirroring, also uses two separate controllers for better performance and reliability. See *Disk Mirroring*.

Disk Mirroring   The process of keeping an exact duplicate of data on two different partitions located on different physical drives. Used for fault tolerance. See *Disk Duplexing*.

Disk Striping   Data that is stored across partitions of identical size on different drives. Also referred to as RAID 0. See *Redundant Array of Inexpensive Disks*.

Disk Striping with Parity   Disk striping with parity distributed across the stripe set for fault tolerance features. Also referred to as RAID 5. See *Stripe Set*, *Redundant Array of Inexpensive Disks*.

DLC   See *Data Link Control*.

DNS   See *Domain Name Service*.

Domain   In Microsoft networks, a domain is an arrangement of client and server computers referenced by a specific name that share a single security permissions database. On the Internet, a domain is a named collection of hosts and subdomains, registered with a unique name by the InterNIC. See *Workgroup*, *InterNIC*.

Domain Controllers   Servers that authenticate workstation network logon requests by comparing a username and password against account information stored in the user accounts database. A user cannot access a domain without authentication from a domain controller. See *Primary Domain Controller*, *Backup Domain Controller, Domain*.

Domain Name   The textual identifier of a specific Internet Host. Domain names are in the form of **server.organization.type** (**www.microsoft.com**) and are resolved to Internet addresses by Domain Name Servers. See *Domain Name Server*.

Domain Name Server   An Internet host dedicated to the function of translating fully qualified domain names into IP addresses. See *Domain Name*.

Domain Name Service (DNS)   The TCP/IP network service that translates textual Internet network addresses into numerical Internet network addresses. See *TCP/IP, Internet*.

Drive   See *Hard Disk Drive*.

Drive Letters   Single letters assigned as abbreviations to the mass storage volumes available to a computer. See *Volumes*.

Driver   A program that provides a software interface to a hardware device. Drivers are written for the specific device they control, but they present a common software interface to the computer's operating system, allowing all devices (of a similar type) to be controlled as if they were the same. See *Data Link Layer, Operating System*.

Dynamic Data Exchange (DDE)   A method of interprocess communication within the Microsoft Windows operating systems.

Dynamic Host Configuration Protocol (DHCP)   DHCP is a method of automatically assigning IP addresses to client computers on a network.

Electronic Mail (e-mail)   A type of client/server application that provides a routed, stored-message service between any two user e-mail accounts. E-mail accounts are not the same as user accounts, but a one-to-one relationship usually exists between them. Because all modern computers can attach to the Internet, users can send e-mail over the Internet to any location that has telephone or wireless digital service. See *Internet*.

Emergency Repair Disk   A disk containing the critical system files (such as portions of the Registry, the **autoexec.bat** file, and the **config.sys** file) necessary to recover your NT machine in some cases.

Encryption   The process of obscuring information by modifying it according to a mathematical function known only to the intended recipient. Encryption secures information being transmitted over nonsecure or untrusted media. See *Security*.

Enterprise Network   A complex network consisting of multiple servers and multiple domains over a large geographic area.

Environment Variables   Variables, such as the search path, that contain information available to programs and batch files about the current operating system environment.

ERD   See *Emergency Repair Disk.*

Ethernet   The most popular Data Link-layer standard for local area networking. Ethernet implements the carrier sense multiple access with collision detection (CSMA/CD) method of arbitrating multiple computer access to the same network. This standard supports the use of Ethernet over any type of media including wireless broadcast. Standard Ethernet operates as 10 megabits per second. Fast Ethernet operates at 100 megabits per second. See *Data Link Layer.*

Exchange   Microsoft's messaging application. Exchange implements Microsoft's mail application programming interface (MAPI) as well as other messaging protocols such as POP, SNMP, and faxing to provide a flexible message composition and reception service. See *Electronic Mail, Fax Modem.*

Explorer   The default shell for Windows 95 and Windows NT 4.0. Explorer implements the more flexible desktop objects paradigm rather than the Program Manager paradigm used in earlier versions of Windows. See *Desktop.*

FAT   See *File Allocation Table.*

Fault Tolerance   Any method that prevents system failure by tolerating single faults, usually through hardware redundancy.

Fax Modems   Special modems that include hardware to allow the transmission and reception of facsimiles. See *Modem, Exchange.*

FDDI   See *Fiber Distributed Data Interface.*

Fiber Distributed Data Interface (FDDI)   A Data Link layer that implements two counter-rotating token rings at 100 megabits per second. FDDI was a popular standard for interconnecting campus and metropolitan area networks because it allows distant digital connections at high speed, but ATM is replacing FDDI in many sites. See *Asynchronous Transfer Mode, Data Link Layer.*

File Allocation Table (FAT)   The file system used by MS-DOS and available to other operating systems such as Windows (all versions), OS/2, and the Macintosh. FAT has become something of a mass storage compatibility standard because of its simplicity and wide availability. FAT has few fault tolerance features and can become corrupted through normal use over time. See *File System*.

File Attributes   Bits stored along with the name and location of a file in a directory entry that show the status of a file, such as archived, hidden, read-only, etc. Different operating systems use different file attributes to implement such services as sharing, compression, and security.

File System   A software component that manages the storage of files on a mass storage device by providing services that can create, read, write, and delete files. File systems impose an ordered database of files on the mass storage device, called volumes, that use hierarchies of directories to organize files. See *Mass Storage Device, Files, Database, Volumes, Directories*.

File Transfer Protocol (FTP)   A simple Internet protocol that transfers complete files from an FTP server to a client running the FTP client. FTP provides a simple no-overhead method of transferring files between computers but cannot perform browsing functions. You must know the URL of the FTP server to which you wish to attach. See *Internet, Uniform Resource Locator*.

Files   A set of data stored on a mass storage device identified by a directory entry containing a name, file attributes, and the physical location of the file in the volume. See *Volume, Mass Storage Device, Directory, File Attributes*.

Firmware   Software stored permanently in nonvolatile memory and built into a computer to provide its BIOS and a bootstrap routine. Simple computers may have their entire operating system built into firmware. See *BIOS, Boot, Software*.

Format   The process of preparing a mass storage device for use with a file system. There are actually two levels of formatting. Low-level formatting writes a structure of sectors and tracks to the disk with bits used by the mass storage controller hardware. The controller hardware requires this format, and it is independent of the file system. High-level formatting creates file system structures such as an allocation table and a root directory in a partition, thus creating a volume. See *Mass Storage Device, Volume*.

Frame   A data structure that network hardware devices use to transmit data between computers. Frames consist of the addresses of the sending and receiving computers, size information, and a check sum. Frames are envelopes around packets of data that allow the packets to be addressed to specific computers on a shared media network. See *Ethernet, FDDI, Token Ring*.

FTP   See *File Transfer Protocol*.

Gateway   A computer that serves as a router, a format translator, or a security filter for an entire network.

Gateway Services for NetWare (GSNW)   An NT Server service that is used to connect NT Servers and NT clients to NetWare resources via the gateway software. See *Gateway, NetWare, Client Services for NetWare*.

GDI   See *Graphical Device Interface*.

Global Group   A special group that only exists on NT Server domain controllers. A global group can only contain members from within its domain. See *Local Group*.

Gopher   Serves text and links to other Gopher sites. Gopher pre-dates HTTP by about a year, but has been made obsolete by the richer format provided by HTTP. See *Hypertext Transfer Protocol*.

Graphical Device Interface (GDI)   The programming interface and graphical services provided to Win32 for programs to interact with graphical devices such as the screen and printer. See *Programming Interface, Win32*.

Graphical User Interface (GUI)   A computer shell program that represents mass storage devices, directories, and files as graphical objects on a screen. A cursor driven by a pointing device such as a mouse manipulates the objects. See *Shell, Explorer*.

Group Identifiers   Security identifiers that contain the set of permissions given to a group. When a user account is part of a group, the group identifier is appended to that user's security identifier, thus granting the individual user all the permissions assigned to that group. See *Security Identifier, Accounts, Permissions*.

Groups Security entities to which users can be assigned membership for the purpose of applying the broad set of group permissions to the user. By managing permissions for groups and assigning users to groups, rather than assigning permissions to users, security administrators can keep coherent control of very large security environments. See *Permissions, Accounts, Security, Local Group, Global Group.*

GSNW See *Gateway Services for NetWare.*

GUI See *Graphical User Interface.*

HAL See *Hardware Abstraction Layer.*

Hard Disk See *Hard Disk Drives.*

Hard Disk Drives Mass storage devices that read and write digital information magnetically on discs that spin under moving heads. Hard disk drives are precisely aligned and cannot normally be removed. Hard disk drives are an inexpensive way to store gigabytes of computer data permanently. Hard disk drives also store the installed software of a computer. See *Mass Storage Device.*

Hardware Abstraction Layer (HAL) A Windows NT service that provides basic input/output services such as timers, interrupts, and multiprocessor management for computer hardware. The HAL is a device driver for the motherboard circuitry that allows different families of computers to be treated the same by the Windows NT operating system. See *Driver, Service, Interrupt Request.*

Hardware Compatibility List (HCL) The listing of all hardware devices supported by Windows NT. Hardware on the HCL has been tested and verified as being compatible with NT. You can view the current HCL at **http:// microsoft.com/ntserver/hcl.**

Hardware Profiles Used to manage portable computers which have different configurations based on their location.

HCL See *Hardware Compatibility List.*

High Performance File System (HPFS) The file system native to OS/2 that performs many of the same functions of NTFS when run under OS/2. See *File System, New Technology File System.*

Home Directory   A directory used to store users' personal files and programs.

Home Page   The default page returned by an HTTP server when a URL containing no specific document is requested. See *Hypertext Transfer Protocol, Uniform Resource Locator.*

Host   An Internet Server. Hosts are constantly connected to the Internet. See *Internet.*

HPFS   See *High Performance File System.*

HTML   See *Hypertext Markup Language.*

HTTP   See *Hypertext Transfer Protocol.*

Hyperlink   A link embedded in text or graphics that has a Web address embedded in it. By clicking the link, you jump to another Web address. You can identify a hyperlink because it is a different color from the rest of the Web page. See *World Wide Web.*

Hypertext Markup Language (HTML)   A textual data format that identifies such sections of a document as headers, lists, hypertext links, etc. HTML is the data format used on the World Wide Web for the publication of Web pages. See *Hypertext Transfer Protocol, World Wide Web.*

Hypertext Transfer Protocol (HTTP)   Hypertext transfer protocol is an Internet protocol that transfers HTML documents over the Internet and responds to context changes that happen when a user clicks on a hypertext link. See *Hypertext Markup Language, World Wide Web.*

Icon   A graphical representation of a resource (in a graphical user interface) that usually takes the form of a small (32 × 32) bitmap. See *Graphical User Interface.*

IDE   A simple mass storage device interconnection bus that operates at 5Mbps and can handle no more than two attached devices. IDE devices are similar to but less expensive than SCSI devices. See *Small Computer Systems Interface, Mass Storage Device.*

IIS   See *Internet Information Server.*

Industry Standard Architecture (ISA)   The design standard for 16-bit Intel compatible motherboards and peripheral buses. The 32/64-bit PCI bus standard is replacing the ISA standard. Adapters and interface cards must conform to the bus standard(s) used by the motherboard in order to be used with a computer.

Integrated Services Digital Network (ISDN)   A direct, digital dial-up PSTN Data Link-layer connection that operates at 64KB per channel over regular twisted pair cable between a subscriber site and a PSTN central office. ISDN provides twice the data rate of the fastest modems per channel. Up to 24 channels can be multiplexed over two twisted pairs. See *Public Switched Telephone Network, Data Link Layer, Modem.*

Intel Architecture   A family of microprocessors descended from the Intel 8086, itself descended from the first microprocessor, the Intel 4004. The Intel architecture is the dominant microprocessor family. It was used in the original IBM PC microcomputer adopted by the business market and later adapted for home use.

Interactive User   A user who physically logs on to the computer where the user account resides is considered interactive, as opposed to a user who logs in over the network. See *Network User.*

Internet   A voluntarily interconnected global network of computers based upon the TCP/IP protocol suite. TCP/IP was originally developed by the U.S. Department of Defense's Advanced Research Projects Agency to facilitate the interconnection of military networks and was provided free to universities. The obvious utility of worldwide digital network connectivity and the availability of free complex networking software developed at universities doing military research attracted other universities, research institutions, private organizations, businesses, and finally the individual home user. The Internet is now available to all current commercial computing platforms. See *FTP, Telnet, World Wide Web, TCP/IP.*

Internet Explorer   A World Wide Web browser produced by Microsoft and included free with Windows 95 and Windows NT 4.0. See *World Wide Web, Internet.*

Internet Information Server (IIS)   Serves Internet higher level protocols like HTTP and FTP to clients using Web browsers. See *Hypertext Transfer Protocol, File Transfer Protocol, and World Wide Web.*

Internet Protocol (IP)   The Network layer protocol upon which the Internet is based. IP provides a simple connectionless packet exchange. Other protocols such as UDP or TCP use IP to perform their connection-oriented or guaranteed delivery services. See *TCP/IP, Internet.*

Internet Service Provider (ISP)   A company that provides dial-up connections to the Internet. See *Internet.*

Internetwork Packet eXchange (IPX)   The Network and Transport layer protocol developed by Novell for its NetWare product. IPX is a routable, connection-oriented protocol similar to TCP/IP but much easier to manage and with lower communication overhead. See *IP, NetWare, NWLink.*

InterNIC   The agency that is responsible for assigning IP addresses. See *Internet Protocol, IP Address.*

Interprocess Communications (IPC)   A generic term describing any manner of client/server communication protocol, specifically those operating in the application layer. Interprocess communications mechanisms provide a method for the client and server to trade information. See *Named Pipes, Remote Procedure Call, NetBIOS, Mailslots, NetDDE, Local Procedure Call.*

Interrupt Request (IRQ)   A hardware signal from a peripheral device to the microcomputer indicating that it has I/O traffic to send. If the microprocessor is not running a more important service, it will interrupt its current activity and handle the interrupt request. IBM PCs have 16 levels of interrupt request lines. Under Windows NT each device must have a unique interrupt request line. See *Microprocessor, Driver, Peripheral.*

Intranet   A privately owned network based on the TCP/IP protocol suite. See *Transmission Control Protocol/Internet Protocol.*

IP   See *Internet Protocol.*

IP Address   A 4-byte number that uniquely identifies a computer on an IP internetwork. InterNIC assigns the first bytes of Internet IP addresses and administers them in hierarchies. Huge organizations like the government or top-level ISPs have class A addresses, large organizations and most ISPs have class B addresses, and small companies have class C addresses. In a class A address, InterNIC assigns the first byte, and the owning organization assigns the remaining three bytes. In a class B address, InterNIC or the higher level ISP assigns the first two bytes, and the organization assigns the remaining two bytes. In a class C address, InterNIC or the higher level ISP assigns the first three bytes , and the organization assigns the remaining byte. Organizations not attached to the Internet are free to assign IP addresses as they please. See *IP, Internet, InterNIC*.

IPC   See *Interprocess Communications*.

IPX   See *Internetwork Packet eXchange*.

IRQ   See *Interrupt Request*.

ISA   See *Industry Standard Architecture*.

ISDN   See *Integrated Services Digital Network*.

ISP   See *Internet Service Provider*.

Kernel   The core process of a preemptive operating system, consisting of a multitasking scheduler and the basic security services. Depending upon the operating system, other services such as virtual memory drivers may be built into the Kernel. The Kernel is responsible for managing the scheduling of threads and processes. See *Operating System, Drivers*.

LAN   See *Local Area Network*.

LAN Manager   The Microsoft brand of a network product jointly developed by IBM and Microsoft that provided an early client/server environment. LAN Manager/Server was eclipsed by NetWare, but was the genesis of many important protocols and IPC mechanisms used today, such as NetBIOS, named pipes, and NetBEUI. Portions of this product exist today in OS/2 Warp Server. See *OS/2, Interprocess Communications*.

LAN Server   The IBM brand of a network product jointly developed by IBM and Microsoft. See *LAN Manager*.

Local Area Network (LAN)   A network of computers operating on the same high-speed, shared media network Data Link layer. The size of a local area network is defined by the limitations of high speed shared media networks to generally less than 1 kilometer in overall span. Some LAN backbone Data Link-layer protocols such as FDDI can create larger LANs called metropolitan or medium area networks (MANs). See *Wide Area Network, Data Link Layer*.

Local Group   A group that exists in an NT computer's local accounts database. Local groups can reside on NT Workstations or NT Servers and can contain users or global groups. See *Global Group*.

Local Printer   A local printer is a printer that uses a physical port and has not been shared. If a printer is defined as local, the only users who can use the printer are the local users of the computer that the printer is attached to. See *Printer, Printing Device, Network Printer*.

Local Procedure Call (LPC)   A mechanism that loops remote procedure calls without the presence of a network so that the client and server portion of an application can reside on the same machine. Local procedure calls look like remote procedure calls (RPCs) to the client and server sides of a distributed application. See *Remote Procedure Call*.

Local Security   Security that governs a local or interactive user. Local security can be set through NTFS partitions. See *Security, Interactive User, New Technology File System, Network Security*.

LocalTalk   A Data Link-layer standard for local area networking used by Macintosh computers. LocalTalk is available on all Macintosh computers. The drawback of LocalTalk is that it only transmits at 230.4 kilobits per second (as opposed to Ethernet which can transmit at 10 megabits per second). See *Data Link Layer, Macintosh*.

Logging   The process of recording information about activities and errors in the operating system.

Logical Port   Printers can be attached to a network through a logical port. A logical port uses a direct connection to gain access to the network. This is done by installing a network card on the printer. The advantages to using logical ports are that they are much faster than physical ports and that you are not limited to the cabling limitations imposed by parallel and serial cable distances allowed when connecting a printer to a PC's parallel or serial ports. See *Printer, Printing Device*.

Logoff   The process of closing an open session with a server. See *Logon*.

Logon   The process of opening a network session by providing a valid authentication consisting of a user account name and a password to a domain controller. After logon, network resources are available to the user according to the user's assigned permissions. See *Domain Controller, Logoff*.

Logon Script   Command files that automate the logon process by performing utility functions such as attaching to additional server resources or automatically running different programs based upon the user account that established the logon. See *Logon*.

Long Filename (LFN)   A filename longer than the eight characters plus three-character extension allowed by MS-DOS. In Windows NT and Windows 95, long filenames may be up to 255 characters.

LPC   See *Local Procedure Call*.

Macintosh   A brand of computer manufactured by Apple Computers, Inc. Macintosh is the only successful line of computers neither based upon the original IBM PC nor running the UNIX operating system. Windows NT Server supports Apple computers despite their use of proprietary network protocols.

MacOS   The operating system that runs on an Apple Macintosh computer. See *Macintosh*.

Mailslots   A connectionless messaging IPC mechanism that Windows NT uses for browse request and logon authentication. See *Interprocess Communications*.

Mandatory User Profile   A profile created by an administrator and saved with a special extension (**.man**) so that the user cannot modify the profile in any way. Mandatory user profiles can be assigned to a single user or a group of users. See *User Profile*.

Mass Storage Device   Any device capable of storing many megabytes of information permanently, but especially those capable of random access to any portion of the information, such as hard disk drives and CD-ROM drives. See *SCSI, IDE, Hard Disk Drive, CD-ROM Drive*.

Master Browser   A network computer that keeps a list of computers and services available on the network and distributes the list to other browsers. The Master Browser may also promote potential browsers to be browsers. See *Browser, Browsing, Potential Browser, Backup Browser*.

Member Server   An NT server that has been installed as a non-domain controller. This allows the server to operate as a file, print and application server without the overhead of accounts administration.

Memory   Any device capable of storing information. This term is usually used to indicate volatile random access semiconductor memory (RAM) capable of high-speed access to any portion of the memory space, but incapable of storing information without power. See *Random Access Memory, Mass Storage Device*.

Microprocessor   An integrated semiconductor circuit designed to automatically perform lists of logical and arithmetic operations. Modern microprocessors independently manage memory pools and support multiple instruction lists called threads. Microprocessors are also capable of responding to interrupt requests from peripherals and include onboard support for complex floating point arithmetic. Microprocessors must have instructions when they are first powered on. These instructions are contained in nonvolatile firmware called a BIOS. See *BIOS, Operating System*.

Microsoft Disk Operating System (MS-DOS)   A 16-bit operating system designed for the 8086 chip that was used in the original IBM PC. MS-DOS is a simple program loader and file system that turns over complete control of the computer to the running program and provides very little service beyond file system support and that provided by the BIOS.

Migration Tool for NetWare   A utility used to migrate NetWare users, groups, file structures, and security to an NT domain. See *NetWare*.

Modem   Modulator/demodulator. A Data Link layer device used to create an analog signal suitable for transmission over telephone lines from a digital data stream. Modern modems also include a command set for negotiating connections and data rates with remote modems and for setting their default behavior. The fastest modems run at about 33Kbps. See *Data Link Layer*.

Module   A software component of a modular operating system that provides a certain defined service. Modules can be installed or removed depending upon the service requirements of the software running on the computer. Modules allow operating systems and applications to be customized to fit the needs of the user.

MPR   See *MultiProtocol Router*.

MS-DOS   See *Microsoft Disk Operating System*.

Multilink   A capability of RAS to combine multiple data streams into one network connection for the purpose of using more than one modem or ISDN channel in a single connection. This feature is new to Windows NT 4.0. See *Remote Access Service*.

Multiprocessing   Using two or more processors simultaneously to perform a computing task. Depending upon the operating system, processing may be done asymmetrically, wherein certain processors are assigned certain threads independent of the load they create, or symmetrically, wherein threads are dynamically assigned to processors according to an equitable scheduling scheme. The term usually describes a multiprocessing capacity built into the computer at a hardware level in that the computer itself supports more than one processor. However, *multiprocessing* can also be applied to network computing applications achieved through interprocess communication mechanisms. Client/server applications are, in fact, examples of multiprocessing. See *Asymmetrical Multiprocessing, Symmetrical Multiprocessing, Interprocess Communications*.

MultiProtocol Router (MPR)   Services included with NT Server that allow you to route traffic between IPX and TCP/IP subnets. MPR also allows you to facilitate DHCP requests and forward BOOTP relay agents. See *Internetwork Packet Exchange, Transmission Control Protocol/Internet Protocol, Dynamic Host Configuration Protocol, Bootstrap Protocol*.

Multitasking   The capacity of an operating system to switch rapidly among threads of execution. Multitasking divides processor time among threads as if each thread ran on its own slower processor. Multitasking operating systems allow two or more applications to run at the same time and can provide a greater degree of service to applications than single-tasking operating systems like MS-DOS. See *Multiprocessing, Multithreading*.

Named Pipes   An interprocess communication mechanism implemented as a file system service, allowing programs to be modified to run on it without using a proprietary application programming interface. Named pipes were developed to support more robust client/server communications than those allowed by the simpler NetBIOS. See *OS/2, File Systems, Interprocess Communications*.

NDIS   See *Network Driver Interface Specification*.

NDS   See *NetWare Directory Services*.

NetBEUI   See *NetBIOS Extended User Interface*.

NetBIOS   See *Network Basic Input/Output System*.

NetBIOS Extended User Interface (NetBEUI)   A simple Network layer transport protocol developed to support NetBIOS installations. NetBEUI is not routable, and so it is not appropriate for larger networks. NetBEUI is the fastest transport protocol available for Windows NT.

NetBIOS Gateway   A service provided by RAS that allows NetBIOS requests to be forwarded independent of transport protocol. For example, NetBIOS requests from a remote computer connected via NetBEUI can be sent over the network via NWLink. See *Network Basic Input/Output System, NWLink, NetBIOS over TCP/IP, NetBEUI*.

NetBIOS over TCP/IP (NetBT)   A network service that implements the NetBIOS IPC over the TCP/IP protocol stack. See *NetBIOS, Interprocess Communications, TCP/IP*.

NetBT   See *NetBIOS over TCP/IP*.

NetDDE   See *Network Dynamic Data Exchange*.

NetWare   A popular network operating system developed by Novell in the early 1980s. NetWare is a cooperative, multitasking, highly optimized, dedicated-server network operating system that has client support for most major operating systems. Recent versions of NetWare include graphical client tools for management from client stations. At one time, NetWare accounted for more than 70 percent of the network operating system market. See *Windows NT, Client Services for NetWare, Gateway Services for NetWare, NWLink*.

NetWare Directory Services (NDS)   In NetWare a distributed hierarchy of network services such as servers, shared volumes, and printers. NetWare implements NDS as a directory structure having elaborate security and administration mechanisms. The CSNW provided in Windows NT 4.0 supports the NDS tree. See *NetWare, Client Services for NetWare, Gateway Services for NetWare*.

NetWare Link (NWLink)   A Windows NT transport protocol that implements Novell's IPX. NWLink is useful as a general purpose transport for Windows NT and for connecting to NetWare file servers through CSNW. See *Internetwork Packet eXchange, Client Services for NetWare, Gateway Services for NetWare*.

NetWare NetBIOS Link (NWNBLink)   NetBIOS implemented over NWLink. See *NetBIOS, NWLink, NetBT.*

Network   A group of computers connected via some digital medium for the purpose of exchanging information. Networks can be based upon many types of media, such as twisted pair telephone-style cable, optical fiber, coaxial cable, radio, or infrared light. Certain computers are usually configured as service providers called *servers*. Computers that perform user tasks directly and that utilize the services of servers are called *clients*. See *Client/Server, Server, Network Operating System.*

Network Basic Input/Output System (NetBIOS)   A client/server interprocess communication service developed by IBM in the early 1980s. NetBIOS presents a relatively primitive mechanism for communication in client server/ applications, but its widespread acceptance and availability across most operating systems makes it a logical choice for simple network applications. Many of the network IPC mechanisms in Windows NT are implemented over NetBIOS. See *Interprocess Communication, Client/Server.*

Network Client Administrator   A utility within the Administrative Tools group that can be used to make installation startup disks, make installation disk sets, copy client-based administration tools, and view remoteboot information.

Network Driver Interface Specification (NDIS)   A Microsoft specification to which network adapter drivers must conform in order to work with Microsoft network operating systems. NDIS provides a many-to-many binding between network adapter drivers and transport protocols. See *Transport Protocol.*

Network Dynamic Data Exchange (NetDDE)   An interprocess communication mechanism developed by Microsoft to support the distribution of DDE applications over a network. See *Interprocess Communication, DDE.*

Network Interface Card (NIC)   A Physical layer adapter device that allows a computer to connect to and communicate over a local area network. See *Ethernet, Token Ring, Adapter.*

Network Layer   The layer of the OSI model that creates a communication path between two computers via routed packets. Transport protocols implement both the Network layer and the Transport layer of the OSI stack. IP is a Network layer service. See *Internet Protocol, Transport Protocol, Open Systems Interconnect Model.*

Network Monitor   A utility used to capture and display network traffic.

Network Operating System   A computer operating system specifically designed to optimize a computer's ability to respond to service requests. Servers run network operating systems. Windows NT Server and NetWare are both network operating systems. See *Windows NT, Server, NetWare.*

Network Printer   A network printer can use physical or logical ports. By defining a printer as a network printer, you make the printer available to local and network users. See *Printer, Printing Device, Local Printer.*

Network Security   Security that governs a network. See *Security, Network User, Local Security.*

Network User   A user who logs on to the network using the SAM from a remote domain controller. See *Interactive User.*

New Technology File System (NTFS)   A secure, transaction-oriented file system developed for Windows NT that incorporates the Windows NT security model for assigning permissions and shares. NTFS is optimized for hard drives larger than 500MB and requires too much overhead to be used on hard disk drives smaller than 50MB.

Nonbrowser   A computer on a network that will not maintain a list of other computers and services on the network. See *Browser, Browsing.*

NT Directory Services   The synchronized SAM database that exists between the PDC and the BDCs within a domain. Directory Services also controls the trust relationships that exist between domains. See *Security Accounts Manager, Primary Domain Controller, Backup Domain Controller, Trust Relationship.*

NTFS   See *New Technology File System.*

NWLink   See *NetWare Link, Internetwork Packet eXchange.*

NWNBLink   See *NetWare NetBIOS Link.*

Object   A software service provider that encapsulates both the algorithm and the data structures necessary to provide a service. Usually, objects can inherit data and functionality from their parent objects, thus allowing complex services to be constructed from simpler objects. The term *object oriented* implies a tight relationship between algorithms and data structures. See *Module*.

Object Counters   Containers built into each service object in Windows NT that store a count of the number of times an object performs its service or to what degree. You can use performance monitors to access object counters and measure how the different objects in Windows NT are operating. See *Object*.

Open Graphics Language (OpenGL)   A standard interface for the presentation of two- and three-dimensional visual data.

Open Systems Interconnect Model (OSI Model)   A model for network component interoperability developed by the International Standards Organization to promote cross-vendor compatibility of hardware and software network systems. The OSI model splits the process of networking into seven distinct services. Each layer uses the services of the layer below to provide its service to the layer above. See *Physical Layer, Data Link Layer, Network Layer, Transport Layer, Session Layer, Presentation Layer, Application Layer*.

OpenGL   See *Open Graphics Language*.

Operating System   A collection of services that form a foundation upon which applications run. Operating systems may be simple I/O service providers with a command shell, such as MS-DOS, or they may be sophisticated, preemptive, multitasking, multiprocessing applications platforms like Windows NT. See *Network Operating System, Preemptive Multitasking, Kernel*.

Operating System 2 (OS/2)   A 16-bit (and later, 32-bit) operating system developed jointly by Microsoft and IBM as a successor to MS-DOS. Microsoft bowed out of the 32-bit development effort and produced its own product, Windows NT, as a competitor to OS/2. OS/2 is now a preemptive, multitasking 32-bit operating system with strong support for networking and the ability to run MS-DOS and Win16 applications, but IBM has been unable to entice a large number of developers to produce software that runs native under OS/2. See *Operating System, Preemptive Multitasking*.

Optimization   Any effort to reduce the workload on a hardware component by eliminating, obviating, or reducing the amount of work required of the hardware component through any means. For instance, file caching is an optimization that reduces the workload of a hard disk drive.

OS/2   See *Operating System 2.*

OSI Model   See *Open Systems Interconnect Model.*

Owner   Used in conjunction with NTFS volumes. All NTFS files and directories have an associated owner who is able to control access and grant permissions to other users. See *New Technology File System.*

Page File   See *Swap File.*

Partition   A section of a hard disk that can contain an independent file system volume. Partitions can be used to keep multiple operating systems and file systems on the same hard disk. See *Volume, Hard Disk Drive.*

Password   A secret code used to validate the identity of a user of a secure system. Passwords are used in tandem with account names to log on to most computer systems.

PC   See *Personal Computer.*

PCI   See *Peripheral Connection Interface.*

PDC   See *Primary Domain Controller.*

Peer   A networked computer that both shares resources with other computers and accesses the shared resources of other computers. A nondedicated server. See *Server, Client.*

Performance Monitor   A utility provided with NT that provides graphical statistics that can be used to measure performance on your computer.

Peripheral   An input/output device attached to a computer. Peripherals can be printers, hard disk drives, monitors, and so on.

Peripheral Connection Interface (PCI)   A high speed 32/64-bit bus interface developed by Intel and widely accepted as the successor to the 16-bit ISA interface. PCI devices support I/O throughput about 40 times faster than the ISA bus.

Permissions   Security constructs used to regulate access to resources by user name or group affiliation. Permissions can be assigned by administrators to allow any level of access, such as read only, read/write, delete, etc., by controlling the ability of users to initiate object services. Security is implemented by checking the user's security identifier against each object's access control list. See *Security Identifier, Access Control List.*

Personal Computer (PC)   A microcomputer used by one person at a time (not a multiuser computer). PCs are generally clients or peers in a networked environment. High-speed PCs are called workstations. Networks of PCs are called local area networks. The term PC is often used to refer to computers compatible with the IBM PC.

Physical Layer   The cables, connectors, and connection ports of a network. The passive physical components required to create a network. See *OSI Model.*

Physical Port   Printers can be connected directly to a computer through a serial (COM) or parallel (LPT) port. If a printer is connected in this manner, it is using a physical port. See *Printer, Print Device.*

Point-to-Point Protocol (PPP)   A Network-layer transport that performs over point-to-point network connections such as serial or modem lines. PPP can negotiate any transport protocol used by both systems involved in the link and can automatically assign IP, DNS, and gateway addresses when used with TCP/IP. See *Internet Protocol, Domain Name Service, Gateway.*

Point-to-Point Tunneling Protocol (PPTP)   Protocol used to connect to corporate networks through the Internet or an ISP. See *Internet, Internet Service Provider.*

Policies   General controls that enhance the security of an operating environment. In Windows NT, policies affect restrictions on password use and rights assignment and determine which events will be recorded in the Security log.

Potential Browser   A computer on a network that may maintain a list of other computers and services on the network if requested to do so by a Master Browser. See *Browser, Master Browser.*

PowerPC   A microprocessor family developed by IBM to compete with the Intel family of microprocessors. The PowerPC is a RISC-architecture microprocessor with many advanced features that emulate other microprocessors. PowerPCs are currently used in a line of IBM computers and in the Apple Power Macintosh. Windows NT is available for the PowerPC.

PPP   See *Point-to-Point Protocol.*

PPTP   See *Point-to-Point Tunneling Protocol.*

Preemptive Multitasking   A multitasking implementation in which an interrupt routine in the Kernel manages the scheduling of processor time among running threads. The threads themselves do not need to support multitasking in any way because the microprocessor will preempt the thread with an interrupt, save its state, update all thread priorities according to its scheduling algorithm, and pass control to the highest priority thread awaiting execution. Because of the preemptive nature of the implementation, a thread that crashes will not affect the operation of other executing threads. See *Kernel, Thread, Operating System, Process.*

Preferences   Characteristics of user accounts, such as password, profile location, home directory, and logon script.

Presentation Layer   The layer of the OSI model that converts and translates (if necessary) information between the Session and Application layers. See *OSI Model.*

Primary Domain Controller (PDC)   The domain server that contains the master copy of the security, computer, and user accounts databases and that can authenticate workstations. The PDC can replicate its databases to one or more backup domain controllers. The PDC is usually also the Master Browser for the domain. See *Backup Domain Controller, Domain, Master Browser.*

Print Device   A print device is the actual physical printer or hardware device you will print to. See *Printer.*

Print Driver   Each printing device has it's own command set. The print driver is the specific software that understands your print device. Each print device has an associated print driver. See *Print Device.*

Print Processor   Once a print job has been sent to the spooler, the print processor looks at the print job and determines whether or not the job needs further processing. The processing (also called rendering) is used to format the print job so that it can print correctly at the print device. See *Print Spooler*.

Print Server   Print servers are the computers on which the printers have been defined. When you send a job to a network printer, you are actually sending it to the print server first. See *Printer, Print Device*.

Print Spooler (Print Queue)   The print spooler is a directory or folder on the Print Server that actually stores the print jobs until they can be printed. It's very important that your Print Server and Print Spooler have enough hard disk space to hold all of the print jobs that could be pending at any given time. See *Print Server*.

Printer   In NT terminology, a printer is the software interface between the physical printer (see print device) and the operating system. You can create printers through the Printers folder. See *Print Device*.

Printing Pool   Printing pools are created when you have more than one printing device associated with a single printer. Printing pools can be used when you have printers that all use the same print driver that are in the same location. By using printing pools, you are then able to send your print job to the first available printer. See *Printer, Print Device*.

Priority   A level of execution importance assigned to a thread. In combination with other factors, the priority level determines how often that thread will get computer time according to a scheduling algorithm. See *Preemptive Multitasking*.

Process   A running program containing one or more threads. A process encapsulates the protected memory and environment for its threads.

Processor   A circuit designed to automatically perform lists of logical and arithmetic operations. Unlike microprocessors, processors may be designed from discrete components rather than be a monolithic integrated circuit. See *Microprocessor*.

Program   A list of processor instructions designed to perform a certain function. A running program is called a process. A package of one or more programs and attendant data designed to meet a certain application is called software. See *Software, Application, Process, Microprocessor.*

Programming Interfaces   Interprocess communications mechanisms that provide certain high-level services to running processes. Programming interfaces may provide network communication, graphical presentation, or any other type of software service. See *Interprocess Communication.*

Protocol   An established rule of communication adhered to by the parties operating under it. Protocols provide a context in which to interpret communicated information. Computer protocols are rules used by communicating devices and software services to format data in a way that all participants understand. See *Transport Protocol.*

PSTN   See *Public Switched Telephone Network.*

Public Switched Telephone Network (PSTN)   A global network of interconnected digital and analog communication links originally designed to support voice communication between any two points in the world, but quickly adapted to handle digital data traffic when the computer revolution occurred. In addition to its traditional voice support role, the PSTN now functions as the Physical layer of the Internet by providing dial-up and leased lines for the interconnections. See *Internet, Modem, Physical Layer.*

RAID   See *Redundant Array of Inexpensive Disks.*

RAID Controllers   Hard disk drive controllers that implement RAID in hardware. See *Redundant Array of Inexpensive Disks.*

RAM   See *Random Access Memory.*

Random Access Memory (RAM)   Integrated circuits that store digital bits in massive arrays of logical gates or capacitors. RAM is the primary memory store for modern computers, storing all running software processes and contextual data. See *Microprocessor.*

RARP   See *Reverse Address Resolution Protocol.*

RAS   See *Remote Access Service.*

Real-Time Application   A process that must respond to external events at least as fast as those events can occur. Real-time threads must run at very high priorities to ensure their ability to respond in real time. See *Process*.

Redirector   A software service that redirects user file I/O requests over the network. Novell implements the Workstation service and Client services for NetWare as redirectors. Redirectors allow servers to be used as mass storage devices that appear local to the user. See *Client Services for NetWare, File System*.

Reduced Instruction Set Computer (RISC)   A microprocessor technology that implements fewer and more primitive instructions than typical microprocessors and can therefore be implemented quickly with the most modern semiconductor technology and speeds. Programs written for RISC microprocessors require more instructions (longer programs) to perform the same task as a normal microprocessor but are capable of a greater degree of optimization and therefore usually run faster. See *Microprocessor*.

Redundant Array of Inexpensive Disks (RAID)   A group of hard disk drives, coordinated by a special controller, that appears as one physical disk to a computer but stores its data across all the disks to take advantage of the speed and/or fault tolerance afforded by using more than one disk. RAID disk storage has several levels, including 0 (striping), 1 (mirroring), and 5 (striping with parity). RAID systems are typically used for very large storage volumes or to provide fault-tolerance features such as hot swapping of failed disks or automatically backing up data onto replacement disks.

Registry   A database of settings required and maintained by Windows NT and its components. The Registry contains all of the configuration information used by the computer. It is stored as a hierarchical structure and is made up of keys, hives, and value entries. You can use the Registry Editor (REGEDT32 command) to change these settings.

Remote Access Service (RAS)   A service that allows network connections to be established over PSTN lines with modems. The computer initiating the connection is called the RAS client; the answering computer is called the RAS host. See *Modem, Public Switched Telephone Network*.

Remote Procedure Calls (RPC)   A network interprocess communication mechanism that allows an application to be distributed among many computers on the same network. See *Local Procedure Call, Interprocess Communications.*

Remoteboot   The remoteboot service is used to start diskless workstations over the network.

Requests for Comments (RFCs)   The set of standards defining the Internet protocols as determined by the Internet Engineering Task Force and available in the public domain on the Internet. RFCs define the functions and services provided by each of the many Internet protocols. Compliance with the RFCs guarantees cross-vendor compatibility. See *Internet.*

Resource   Any useful service, such as a shared network directory or a printer. See *Share.*

Reverse Address Resolution Protocol (RARP)   The TCP/IP protocol which allows a computer that has a Physical-layer address (such as an Ethernet address), but does not have an IP address to request a numeric IP address from another computer on the network. See *TCP/IP.*

RFC   See *Request For Comments.*

RIP   See *Routing Information Protocol.*

RISC   See *Reduced Instruction Set Computer.*

Roaming User Profile   A user profile that is stored and configured to be downloaded from a server. The purpose of roaming user profiles is that they allow a user to access their profile from any location on the network. See *User Profile.*

Router   A Network layer device that moves packets between networks. Routers provide internetwork connectivity. See *Network Layer.*

Routing Information Protocol (RIP)   A protocol within the TCP/IP protocol suite that allows routers to exchange routing information with other routers. See *Transmission Control Protocol/Internet Protocol.*

RPC   See *Remote Procedure Calls.*

SAM   See *Security Accounts Manager.*

Scheduling   The process of determining which threads should be executed according to their priority and other factors. See *Preemptive Multitasking*.

SCSI   See *Small Computer Systems Interface*.

Search Engine   Web sites dedicated to responding to requests for specific information, searching massive locally stored databases of Web pages, and responding with the URLs of pages that fit the search phrase. See *World Wide Web, Universal Resource Locator*.

Security   The Measures taken to secure a system against accidental or intentional loss, usually in the form of accountability procedures and use restriction. See *Security Identifiers, Security Accounts Manager*.

Security Accounts Manager (SAM)   The module of the Windows NT executive that authenticates a username and password against a database of accounts, generating an access token that includes the user's permissions. See *Security, Security Identifier, Access Token*.

Security Identifiers (SID)   Unique codes that identify a specific user or group to the Windows NT security system. Security identifiers contain a complete set of permissions for that user or group.

Serial   A method of communication that transfers data across a medium one bit at a time, usually adding stop, start, and check bits to ensure quality transfer. See *COM Port, Modem*.

Serial Line Internet Protocol (SLIP)   An implementation of the IP protocol over serial lines. SLIP has been obviated by PPP. See *Point-to-Point Protocol, Internet Protocol*.

Server   A computer dedicated to servicing requests for resources from other computers on a network. Servers typically run network operating systems such as Windows NT Server or NetWare. See *Windows NT, NetWare, Client/ Server*.

Server Manager   Utility in the Administrative Tools group used to manage domains and computers.

Service   A process dedicated to implementing a specific function for another process. Most Windows NT components are services used by User-level applications.

Services for Macintosh   A service available through NT Server that allows Macintosh users to take advantage of NT file and print services. See *Macintosh*.

Session Layer   The layer of the OSI model dedicated to maintaining a bidirectional communication connection between two computers. The Session layer uses the services of the Transport layer to provide this service. See *OSI Model, Transport Layer*.

Share   A resource (e.g., directory, printer) shared by a server or a peer on a network. See *Resource, Server, Peer*.

Shell   The user interface of an operating system; the shell launches applications and manages file systems.

SID   See *Security Identifier*.

Simple Mail Transfer Protocol (SMTP)   An Internet protocol for transferring mail between Internet Hosts. SMTP is often used to upload mail directly from the client to an Intermediate host, but can only be used to receive mail by computers constantly connected to the Internet. See *Internet*.

Simple Network Management Protocol (SNMP)   An Internet protocol that manages network hardware such as routers, switches, servers, and clients from a single client on the network. See *Internet Protocol*.

Site   A related collection of HTML documents at the same Internet address, usually oriented toward some specific information or purpose. See *Hypertext Markup Language, Internet*.

SLIP   See *Serial Line Internet Protocol*.

Small Computer Systems Interface (SCSI)   A high-speed, parallel-bus interface that connects hard disk drives, CD-ROM drives, tape drives, and many other peripherals to a computer. SCSI is the mass storage connection standard among all computers except IBM compatibles, which use SCSI or IDE.

SMTP   See *Simple Mail Transfer Protocol*.

SNMP   See *Simple Network Management Protocol*.

Software   A suite of programs sold as a unit and dedicated to a specific application. See *Program, Application, Process*.

Spooler   A service that buffers output to a low-speed device such as a printer so the software outputting to the device is not tied up waiting for it.

Stripe Set   A single volume created across multiple hard disk drives and accessed in parallel for the purpose of optimizing disk access time. NTFS can create stripe sets. See *NTFS, Volume, File System*.

Subdirectory   A directory contained in another directory. See *Directory*.

Subnet Mask   A number mathematically applied to Internet protocol addresses to determine which IP addresses are a part of the same subnetwork as the computer applying the subnet mask.

Surf   To browse the Web randomly looking for interesting information. See *World Wide Web*.

Swap File   The virtual memory file on a hard disk containing the memory pages that have been moved out to disk to increase available RAM. See *Virtual Memory*.

Symmetrical Multiprocessing   A multiprocessing methodology wherein processes are assigned to processors on a fair share basis. This balances the processing load among processors and ensures that no processor will become a bottleneck. Symmetrical Multiprocessing is more difficult to implement than Asymmetrical multiprocessing as certain hardware functions such as interrupt handling must be shared between processors. See *Asymmetrical Multiprocessing, Multiprocessing*.

System Partition   The system partition is the active partition on an Intel-based computer that contains the hardware specific files used to load the NT operating system. See *Partition, Boot Partition*.

System Policy   A policy used to control what a user can do and the users environment. System policies can be applied to a specific user, group, a computer, or all users. System policies work by overwriting current settings in the Registry with the system policy settings. System policies are created through the System Policy Editor. See *Registry, System Policy Editor*.

System Policy Editor   A utility found within the Administrative Tools group used to create system policies. See *System Policies*.

Task Manager An application that manually views and closes running processes. Task Manager can also be used to view CPU and memory statistics. Press Ctrl+Alt+Del to launch the Task Manager.

TCP See *Transmission Control Protocol.*

TCP/IP See *Transmission Control Protocol/Internet Protocol.*

TDI See *Transport Driver Interface.*

Telnet A terminal application that allows a user to log into a multiuser UNIX computer from any computer connected to the Internet. See *Internet.*

Thread A list of instructions running in a computer to perform a certain task. Each thread runs in the context of a process, which embodies the protected memory space and the environment of the threads. Multithreaded processes can perform more than one task at the same time. See *Process, Preemptive Multitasking, Program.*

Throughput The measure of information flow through a system in a specific time frame, usually one second. For instance, 28.8Kbps is the throughput of a modem: 28.8 kilobits per second can be transmitted.

Token Ring The second most popular Data Link-layer standard for local area networking. Token Ring implements the token passing method of arbitrating multiple-computer access to the same network. Token Ring operates at either 4 or 16Mbps. FDDI is similar to Token Ring and operates at 100Mbps. See *Data Link Layer.*

Transmission Control Protocol (TCP) A Transport-layer protocol that implements guaranteed packet delivery using the Internet Protocol (IP). See *TCP/IP, Internet Protocol.*

Transmission Control Protocol/Internet Protocol (TCP/IP) A suite of Internet protocols upon which the global Internet is based. TCP/IP is a general term that can refer either to the TCP and IP protocols used together or to the complete set of Internet protocols. TCP/IP is the default protocol for Windows NT.

Transport Driver Interface (TDI) A specification to which all Windows NT transport protocols must be written in order to be used by higher-level services such as programming interfaces, file systems, and interprocess communications mechanisms. See *Transport Protocol.*

Transport Layer   The OSI model layer responsible for the guaranteed serial delivery of packets between two computers over an internetwork. TCP is the Transport-layer protocol for the TCP/IP transport protocol.

Transport Protocol   A service that delivers discreet packets of information between any two computers in a network. Higher level connection-oriented services are built upon transport protocols. See *TCP/IP, NWLink, NetBEUI, Transport Layer, IP, TCP, Internet.*

Trust Relationship   An administrative link that joins two or more domains. With a trust relationship users can access resources in another domain if they have rights, even if they do not have a user account in the resource domain.

UDP   See *User Datagram Protocol.*

UNC   See *Universal Naming Convention.*

Uniform Resource Locator (URL)   An Internet standard naming convention for identifying resources available via various TCP/IP application protocols. For example, **http://www.microsoft.com** is the URL for Microsoft's World Wide Web server site, while **ftp://gateway.dec.com** is a popular FTP site. A URL allows easy hypertext references to a particular resource from within a document or mail message. See *HTTP, World Wide Web.*

Universal Naming Convention (UNC)   A multivendor, multiplatform convention for identifying shared resources on a network.

UNIX   A multitasking, kernel-based operating system developed at AT&T in the early 1970s and provided (originally) free to universities as a research operating system. Because of its availability and ability to scale down to microprocessor-based computers, UNIX became the standard operating system of the Internet and its attendant network protocols and is the closest approximation to a universal operating system that exists. Most computers can run some variant of the UNIX operating system. See *Multitasking, Internet.*

User Datagram Protocol (UDP)   A non-guaranteed network packet protocol implemented on IP that is far faster than TCP because of its lack of flow-control overhead. UDP can be implemented as a reliable transport when some higher-level protocol (such as NetBIOS) exists to make sure that required data will eventually be retransmitted in local area environments. At the Transport layer of the OSI model, UDP is connectionless service and TCP is connection-oriented service. See *Transmission Control Protocol.*

User Manager for Domains   A Windows NT application that administers user accounts, groups, and security policies at the domain level.

User Profile   Used to save each user's desktop configuration. See *Roaming Profile, Mandatory Profile*.

User Rights Policies   Used to determine what rights users and groups have when trying to accomplish network tasks. User Rights Policies are set through User Manager for Domains. See *User Manager for Domains*.

Username   A user's account name in a logon-authenticated system. See *Security*.

VDM   See *Virtual DOS Machine*.

Virtual DOS Machine (VDM)   The DOS environment created by Windows NT for the execution of DOS and Win16 applications. See *MS-DOS, Win16*.

Virtual Memory   A kernel service that stores memory pages not currently in use on a mass storage device to free up the memory occupied for other uses. Virtual memory hides the memory swapping process from applications and higher level services. See *Swap File, Kernel*.

Volume   A collection of data indexed by directories containing files and referred to by a drive letter. Volumes are normally contained in a single partition, but volume sets and stripe sets extend a single volume across multiple partitions.

WAN   See *Wide Area Network*.

Web Browser   An application that makes HTTP requests and formats the resultant HTML documents for the users. The preeminent Internet Client, most Web browsers understand all standard Internet protocols. See *Hypertext Transfer Protocol, Hypertext Markup Language, Internet*.

Web Page   Any HTML document on an HTTP server. See *Hypertext Transfer Protocol, Hypertext Markup Language, Internet*.

Wide Area Network (WAN)   A geographically dispersed network of networks, connected by routers and communication links. The Internet is the largest WAN. See *Internet, Local Area Network*.

Win16 The set of application services provided by the 16-bit versions of Microsoft Windows: Windows 3.1 and Windows for Workgroups 3.11.

Win32 The set of application services provided by the 32-bit versions of Microsoft Windows: Windows 95 and Windows NT.

Windows 3.11 for Workgroups The current 16-bit version of Windows for less-powerful, Intel-based personal computers; this system includes peer networking services.

Windows 95 The current 32-bit version of Microsoft Windows for medium-range, Intel-based personal computers; this system includes peer networking services, Internet support, and strong support for older DOS applications and peripherals.

Windows Internet Name Service (WINS) A network service for Microsoft networks that provides Windows computers with Internet numbers for specified NetBIOS names, facilitating browsing and intercommunication over TCP/IP networks.

Windows NT The current 32-bit version of Microsoft Windows for powerful Intel, Alpha, PowerPC, or MIPS-based computers; the system includes peer networking services, server networking services, Internet client and server services, and a broad range of utilities.

Windows Sockets An interprocess communications protocol that delivers connection-oriented data streams used by Internet software and software ported from UNIX environments. See *Interprocess Communications*.

WINS See *Windows Internet Name Service*.

Workgroup In Microsoft networks, a collection of related computers, such as a department, that don't require the uniform security and coordination of a domain. Workgroups are characterized by decentralized management as opposed to the centralized management that domains use. See *Domain*.

Workstation A powerful personal computer, usually running a preemptive, multitasking operating system like UNIX or Windows NT.

World Wide Web (WWW)   A collection of Internet servers providing hypertext formatted documents for Internet clients running Web browsers. The World Wide Web provided the first easy-to-use graphical interface for the Internet and is largely responsible for the Internet's explosive growth.

Write-Back Caching   A caching optimization wherein data written to the slow store is cached until the cache is full or until a subsequent write operation overwrites the cached data. Write-back caching can significantly reduce the write operations to a slow store because many write operations are subsequently obviated by new information. Data in the write-back cache is also available for subsequent reads. If something happens to prevent the cache from writing data to the slow store, the cache data will be lost. See *Caching*, *Write-Through Caching*.

Write-Through Caching   A caching optimization wherein data written to a slow store is kept in a cache for subsequent re-reading. Unlike write-back caching, write-through caching immediately writes the data to the slow store and is therefore less optimal but more secure.

WWW   See *World Wide Web*.

X.25   A Standard that defines packet switching networks.

Index

Note to the Reader: Throughout this index **boldfaced** page numbers indicate primary discussions of a topic. *Italicized* page numbers indicate illustrations.

X

V

W

MCSE CORE REQUIREMENT STUDY GUIDES FROM NETWORK PRESS

Sybex's Network Press expands the definitive study guide series for MCSE candidates.

MCSE: NETWORKING ESSENTIALS STUDY GUIDE SECOND EDITION

ISBN: 0-7821-2220-5
704pp; 7¹/₂" x 9"; Hardcover
$49.99

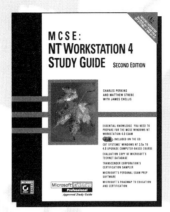

MCSE: NT WORKSTATION 4 STUDY GUIDE SECOND EDITION

ISBN: 0-7821-2223-X
784pp; 7¹/₂" x 9"; Hardcover
$49.99

MCSE: NT SERVER 4 STUDY GUIDE SECOND EDITION

ISBN: 0-7821-2222-1
832pp; 7¹/₂" x 9"; Hardcover
$49.99

MCSE: NT SERVER 4 IN THE ENTERPRISE STUDY GUIDE SECOND EDITION

ISBN: 0-7821-2221-3
704pp; 7¹/₂" x 9"; Hardcover
$49.99

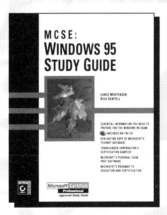

MCSE: WINDOWS 95 STUDY GUIDE

ISBN: 0-7821-2092-X
720pp; 7¹/₂" x 9"; Hardcover
$49.99

A $50.00! SAVINGS

MCSE Core Requirements
Box Set
ISBN: 0-7821-2245-0
4 hardcover books;
3,024pp total; $149.96

STUDY GUIDES FOR THE MICROSOFT CERTIFIED SYSTEMS ENGINEER EXAMS

MCSE ELECTIVE STUDY GUIDES
FROM NETWORK PRESS

Sybex's Network Press expands the definitive study guide series for MCSE candidates.

MCSE: TCP/IP FOR NT SERVER 4 STUDY GUIDE SECOND EDITION

ISBN: 0-7821-2173-X
640pp; 7¹/₂" x 9"; Hardcover
$49.99

MCSE: EXCHANGE 5 STUDY GUIDE

ISBN: 0-7821-1967-0
656pp; 7¹/₂" x 9"; Hardcover
$49.99

MCSE: INTERNET INFORMATION SERVER 3 STUDY GUIDE

ISBN: 0-7821-2110-1
559pp; 7¹/₂" x 9"; Hardcover
$49.99

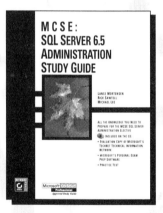

MCSE: SQL SERVER 6.5 ADMINISTRATION STUDY GUIDE

ISBN: 0-7821-2172-1
672pp; 7¹/₂" x 9"; Hardcover
$49.99

MCSE: PROXY SERVER 2 STUDY GUIDE

ISBN: 0-7821-2194-2
576pp; 7¹/₂" x 9"; Hardcover
$49.99

A $25.00! SAVINGS

MCSE Internet Systems
Specialist Box Set
ISBN: 0-7821-2176-4
3 hardcover books;
1,984pp total; $124.97

Microsoft Certified
Professional
Approved Study Guide

NETWORK PRESS
SYBEX

STUDY GUIDES FOR THE MICROSOFT CERTIFIED SYSTEMS ENGINEER EXAMS

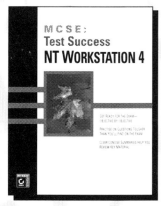

NT® IN THE REAL WORLD

THE INFORMATION YOU NEED TO BUILD, SECURE, AND OPTIMIZE NT® NETWORKS

ISBN: 0-7821-2163-2
1,664 pp; 7¹/₂" x 9"; Hardcover
$59.99

ISBN: 0-7821-2123-3
544 pp; 7¹/₂" x 9"; Softcover
$44.99

ISBN: 0-7821-2006-7
929 pp; 7¹/₂" x 9"; Hardcover
$59.99

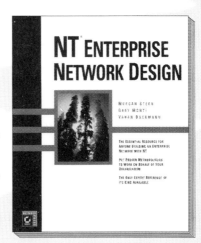

ISBN: 0-7821-2156-X
624 pp; 7¹/₂" x 9"; Hardcover
$54.99

NETWORK PRESS®
SYBEX®